SHOEBURYNESS
A History

Bamford, North Shoebury Hall

SHOEBURYNESS
A History

Judith Williams

Phillimore

2006

Published by
PHILLIMORE & CO. LTD
Shopwyke Manor Barn, Chichester, West Sussex, England
www.phillimore.co.uk

ISBN 1-86077-435-0
ISBN 13 978-1-86077-435-5

Printed and bound in Great Britain by
THE CROMWELL PRESS
Trowbridge, Wiltshire

I have never shot an Elephant, a Buffalo or a Bear,
And I have never tracked a Tiger when it's wounded in its lair.
I have never climbed the Matterhorn or any Alpine Pass
And only once in all my life I've crossed the Mer de Glace.
I've never dared Niagara in a barrel or in a boat,
I'm happier far when I'm on land than when I am afloat.
I have never killed a Lion, like Samson with my hands,
But I've ridden in a market cart across the Maplin Sands.

Sir Francis Carruthers Gould, c.1920

Whisstock, Shore House, 1925

Contents

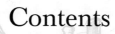

List of Illustrations

Frontispiece: Bamford, North Shoebury Hall, 1919

Acknowledgements

This book would not have been possible without the kind and generous contributions from several people, to whom I am greatly indebted.

In particular, I would like to thank John Askew, Tony Hill and Caroline Gibb, all of who readily gave their time and knowledge. It was a privilege and pleasure to meet them, and their invaluable input to this book is very much appreciated.

I am grateful also for the help of Derek Barber, Tom Mayhew, Joyce Taylor, Valerie Bateson, Derek Everitt and Michelle Palles-Clark. Thank you.

Ken Crowe and his colleagues at Southend Museum, Susan Gough of Southend Central Library, Clare Hunt of Beecroft Art Gallery and the staff of Essex Record Office were all most helpful in the preparation of this book. Thanks to all of them.

Illustrations are reproduced by kind permission of the following: the Beecroft Art Gallery, copyright Southend Museums Service, frontispiece and contents page; Southend Museums Service, 2, 3, 6, 9, 10, 11, 20, 22, 25, 29, 34, 38, 39, 45, 49, 52, 54, 57, 58, 59, 61, 62, 63, 65, 68, 69, 93, 94, 96, 120, 123, 124, 129, 132, 141, 151; Tony Hill, 4, 12, 15, 21, 26, 32, 43, 44, 46, 79, 85, 101, 105, 116, 144; Edward Clack, 5; Phillimore & Co, 13; Janet Purdy (from the Jessie Payne collection), 23, 50; Essex Record Office, 14, 42, 53, 74, 92; Christine Selby, 84; Southend Central Library, 95, 98; www.footstepsphotos.com, 24, 37, 40, 51, 104, 108, 109, 112, 119, 126, 127, 133, 148; Derek Barber, 48, 100, 121; Caroline Gibb, 35, 55, 75, 86, 91, 99, 102, 110, 113, 114, 117, 118, 125, 128, 130, 131, 134, 138; Joyce Taylor, 145. All other illustrations are from the author's own collection.

1   The beach *c.*1905, looking east.

One
Before the Conquest

Shoeburyness lies on the north bank of the Thames estuary, in the extreme south-east corner of Essex; the whole area is an ancient terrace of the River Thames. Low lying and flat, its geology is characterised by gravels laid down by meltwaters and brickearth, a wind-blown clay deposit, dating from the Ice Age.

For thousands of years the coastal region comprised extensive marshes intersected by streams. With regular inundation by the sea causing erosion and loss of land, and possibly occasional gains from deposits, the exact outline of the Shoebury coastline has not been constant over the centuries, and this has affected settlement of the area.

Relatively close to Europe, Shoeburyness was one of the first areas settled by newcomers from the Continent, giving it a long and interesting history. Experts from Southend Museum suspected a rich archaeological source and worked on a 'rescue recording' project north of Elm Road while brickearth was being extracted during the 1970s. A second extensive study of a seven-acre area was conducted from January to November 1981 north-east of St Mary's. Further excavations were carried out on 195 acres of former Ministry of Defence land in South Shoebury in 1998. Previously, many artefacts had been discovered as the brickfields were exploited during the second half of the 19th century, as well as by amateur collectors such as Philip Benton (1815-98) and, to a lesser extent, local schoolmaster N. Hillyer during the 1920s. Specimens from both Hillyer's and Benton's collections now belong to Southend Museum, others to the British Museum. However, only

those artefacts discovered in 1981 or later were assigned any detailed description or dates at the time of collection.

Worked flints and polished axeheads dating back to the Palaeolithic and Mesolithic periods, 3,000 to 2,000 BC, have been discovered in South Shoebury, showing persistent occupation of the area from these early times. However, any firm evidence of an early settlement site is thought to be now buried beneath the North Sea as, at that time, the sea level was some 30-40 metres below the present level. Early humans living in the area would have found plentiful supplies

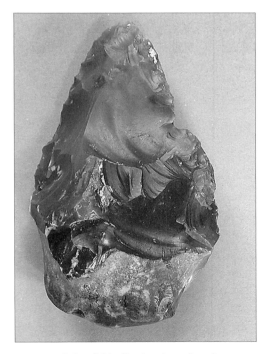

2 Palaeolithic flint hand-axe found at Shoeburyness.

of fish, shellfish and eels, as well as wildfowl, which flourished on the marshes. They would have been familiar with the edible plants that thrive on saltmarshes and mudflats.

Bronze Age

In 1000 BC, the coastline was more-or-less in the form we see today although, west of Shoebury, a huge lagoon covered the area from what is now Southchurch Park to Bournes Green. Distinctive weapons typical of West Alpine people have been found on the fringes of this area, towards Shoebury, and in Shoebury's Bronze-Age hoards.

The earliest human remains in the area are of a Beaker (early Bronze-Age) man found at Thorpe Hall brickfields in 1924 and, in fact, the Shoebury and Thorpe Bay area provides more evidence of Bronze-Age occupation than any other district in the Rochford Hundred.

3 Late Bronze-Age socketed axe head discovered during the 1971 excavations north of Elm Road.

Early, Middle and Late Bronze-Age finds in Shoebury itself indicate long periods of occupation. Indeed, there is evidence of continuous land use from at least the Middle Bronze Age.

The coastal area from Shoeburyness to Leigh-on-Sea appears to have been an important bronze-founding area and a bronze founder's hoard discovered in Shoebury in 1891 came into the possession of Philip Benton; it included 12 socketed celts (axes), an armlet, two palstaves (cutting implements), a winged adze (knife) and portions of other weapons.

A Bronze-Age axehead, together with several flint implements, was found in Richmond Avenue in 1924. Another bronze founder's hoard was discovered in 1930 behind Richmond Avenue school, including two socketed celts, a spearhead, a winged adze and an item thought to be part of a harness fitting.

Proof of Bronze-Age settlement at North Shoebury was uncovered during the 1981 excavations, consisting of small rectilinear enclosures and pits with domestic refuse dating from 1500-1000 BC. Ditches, pits and enclosures indicate settlement and farming activities northeast of St Mary's church in the Middle Bronze Age, continuing until the late Roman period. One irregular gulley with numerous stake holes is thought to be the result of successive erections of temporary fencing. Nearby, a dump of mussel shells was found. Within the enclosures were small clusters of pits and postholes. The settlement may have been a linked group of compounds set within a wider field system. Its siting was no doubt influenced by a springhead, rising just west of St Mary's churchyard, from where water flowed south all the way to the sea. This freshwater stream may have constituted the legendary River Shoe, although there is no evidence that this was ever a navigable waterway. Two cremation burials were unearthed in 1981, one of a woman, south of the main area of settlement, and one of a child, south-east of the settlement.

4 Ness Road, *c.*1920. Daniel Defoe (1659-1731) said that the marshlands pastured 'the best and fattest and the largest veal in England'. However, dairy farming only really took off when the railway arrived in 1854.

By the Middle Bronze Age, sheep, cattle and pigs were kept and probably grazed on the extensive marshland pastures. Carbonised plant remains show that wheat and possibly oats were grown, while the seven cylindrical loom weights found during the 1971 and 1981 excavations indicate the importance of cloth production.

During the Late Bronze Age (1000-600 BC) a more extensive field system developed further to the south and west of the earlier enclosures, but still north-east of St Mary's. Charcoal and burnt clay discovered in 1971-2 indicate a series of hearths in the area, while a trackway ran north-west to south-east, with a ditch nearly parallel to it. A series of post holes south of these suggest a roundhouse with a south-east facing entrance. This is a typical Late Bronze-Age feature, although it may date from the Early Iron Age.

Seven spindle whorls were found, plus some bone objects that were possibly associated with weaving. Sandstone stones probably used for grinding corn were found which, as this is not a local stone, shows that people were deliberately bringing tools to this site. These finds, together with the pottery fragments found – from storage vessels and cooking pots – indicate a domestic situation.

Iron Age

The Iron Age saw a period of developing social organisation. Earthworks were thrown up to protect families and cattle, particularly important for small groups who did not have the protection of a larger tribe. The fertile soils at the mouth of the Thames were attractive to new peoples reaching England from the Continent.

In South Shoebury, an Iron-Age camp has been identified with an overall length of about

5 Aerial view of crop marks off Royal Artillery Way, showing parallel Iron-Age ditches with circular hut within. The irregular dark patterns were formed by ice wedges.

1,500 feet north to south, protected by a semi-circular rampart open to the sea. The banks of this rampart were built 12 feet high and from the points of the crescent extended some 700 feet inland. This prominent feature was long thought to be of Danish origin, but thorough examination in the 1990s proved it to date from the Iron Age. Although the Anglo-Saxon Chronicle records the Danish camp at Shoebury, no artefacts of Danish origin have been found there. Within the rampart, four Iron-Age roundhouses and evidence of trades such as spinning and weaving were found during the 1998 excavations. These, along with cooking vessels found on the site, are thought to have originated in southern England. Pottery finds dating from between 400 and 200 BC suggest that Iron-Age settlers used this camp for up

to 300 years. However, much of the camp and any further archaeological evidence it may have provided has been lost to coastal erosion and, to a lesser degree, to the activities of the garrison firing range. The camp is now a Scheduled Ancient Monument.

During the Iron Age, the 1981 excavations show, the North Shoebury field system, north-east of St Mary's was extensively developed, with associated drove-ways and rectangular enclosures.

A scatter of small pits/postholes and a ditch were discovered. Slightly deeper holes indicate a 10-ft square, four-post structure – possibly a storage facility. A ditch running approximately north-south across the excavated area may have marked a major land division. Other features from this period were a curved gully and a shallow hearth base, which consisted of a scoop lined with burnt brickearth and a large quantity of carbonised peas (a rare find for this period). A ditch which originated in the Late Bronze Age appears to have been re-cut several times, remaining in use as a field boundary into the Early Iron Age, forming one side of a north-west to south-east trackway. Enclosures had been laid out on either side of this central trackway. Traces of two other ditched trackways running roughly parallel were also recorded, with at least one of these leading off towards Wakering.

It is clear that the settlement underwent some changes during this period as pits (probably for storage) occur in the middle of tracks and must have been dug after the tracks went out of use, or vice versa. The presence of spindle whorls and a bone weaving comb indicates the continuation of cloth production. The majority of the pots found appear to have been made locally.

Sections of three Early Iron-Age ovens were found in 1981; these may have been used as kilns. In addition, two round structures were identified as barns and two burials date from this period. Another Iron Age burial was discovered in Elm Road during 1971-2 investigations.

Additional post holes, pits and ditches suggest another Iron-Age site of settlement near Poynters Lane. Known crop marks which may indicate Iron Age roundhouses are two ring ditches and linear features on the north side of Poynters Lane, plus another two ring ditches and a sub-rectangular feature west of North Shoebury Road.

Among the 1981 finds were five complete pots from Early Iron-Age of the Belgic type. It is probable that the area was targeted by Belgic invaders throughout the Iron-Age, although south Essex remained in the control of Celts, most of whom belonged to the powerful Trinovantes tribe. Across Shoebury, pottery is generally of poorer quality than that found in the wealthier north Essex.

In the Middle to Late Iron Age (between 300-50 BC) the Early Iron-Age field system in North Shoebury was abandoned and the settlement shifted further to the west, with a new field system enclosed by a large ditch. A major east-west boundary ditch was dug at this time, forming the southern boundary of a series of smaller north-south ditches. The 1981 excavations show the main centre of occupation to have been immediately north of St Mary's. This settlement may well have extended north, but this cannot be confirmed as that area has not been excavated. Fragments from at least five loom weights were found, suggesting that North Shoebury was particularly associated with cloth production at this time. Pottery remains indicate links to North Kent.

A Late Iron-Age cremation cemetery consisting of three pits in a line, equally spaced seven metres apart and each containing pottery vessels and human bones, was found in 1981 on the eastern edge of the area that had been settled.

A curving gully, possibly forming drainage around a roundhouse, was dated to this period. Outside the gully, a pit contained a human skull, together with the base of a bowl. A

6   Late Iron-Age cremation burial, discovered north-east of St Mary's during the 1981 excavations.

7 Shoebury Common, *c.*1910. Suttons House can just be made out among the trees. The row of elm trees, back left, marks the line of the High Street.

small, shallow pit nearby contained a complete, triangular loom weight.

Remains of animal bones show that cattle were the predominant meat source for the residents of Shoebury, although there were plenty of sheep and/or goats. Pigs were increasingly important from the Late Iron Age.

Romans

A fortified Roman settlement, named Essobiriam, was established in the Shoebury area as early as AD 30. However, as the sea level was some 1.6-2.6 metres lower in Roman times than it is today, evidence of Roman occupation may lie off the current coastline.

Rampart Street is thought to have originally been a Roman track to parts of their settlement (possibly a fort) that are now submerged. Similarly, the 'Broomway' track, linking Wakering Stairs

to Foulness and now just off-shore, may have been a Roman way. This, together with the distribution of Roman finds between Shoebury and Wakering, suggests an extensive Roman settlement.

The existing Iron-Age field system and the north-south ditches in North Shoebury were maintained between AD 43-410, and some new east-west ditches were dug. As the soil was mainly brickearth and gravels, drainage was not the primary function of the ditches – they were probably accompanied by hedges and used as field boundaries. A rectilinear enclosure was built at the eastern boundary of the cultivated area.

Roman artefacts found in North Shoebury were of a greater variety than those dated to earlier periods, including more bricks and tiles. Most 1981 finds were domestic refuse such as bones, shells, as well as some 2,300 fragments of Roman pottery, which come from a minimum of 434 vessels. Much of the second- to third-century pottery appears to have originated at known manufacturing sites in the Nene Valley and Oxfordshire, and much is very similar to that found across the Thames in Kent. This suggests strong communication links, enabling the exchange of goods and ideas. Pottery that can be dated to the fourth century AD includes coarse-ware jars from Rettendon, Northamptonshire and Hertfordshire, together with some local pots.

A long-handled iron ladle was found in 1981, together with a bronze bracelet. Also, part of a bone comb and fragments of a glass vessel.

Other Roman features in North Shoebury, found during the 1981 excavations, were a new track running north-west to south-east. Evidence from animal bones, being mainly of older animals, suggests that sheep were kept for milk or wool as well as meat. Shellfish appear to have been eaten in greater quantities during the Roman period than in earlier times, with oysters accounting for over 50 per cent of the total shells found and it is possible that the Romans cultivated them on the Shoebury shore. Whelks appear for the first time, indicating greater use of the sea.

8 Ness Road junction, c.1905. Ness Road was sometimes called Beach Road.

As in earlier periods, wheat was the most common crop. A flue leading to a chamber appears to have been used for drying corn, while quern stones relate to its processing. It is likely that enough cereal crops, wool, cheese, seafood and salt was produced to allow for trade with other areas.

In South Shoebury in 1990, evidence of a Romano–British building with wattle and daub walls and a tiled roof was found on the site of the garrison Officers' Mess, where coins and pots were found in the 1930s. Remains of salt workings were discovered in Gunners Park.

Roman pottery kilns were discovered on the Shoebury brickfields in the late 19th century, including a near complete kiln (although the pots within it were damaged) discovered near

South Shoebury Hall by labourers in 1895. A stone Roman head was found nearby. The distribution of a number of kilns along the estuary suggests either an itinerant potter or that this was not the potter's main occupation. Other Roman artefacts including cups, pots, urns, domestic utensils and coins have been found north of St Mary's church and beyond it towards Wakering.

The Roman settlement was attacked by the British in AD 50, but survived into the fourth century, although the latest date applicable to the Roman finds is AD 350 and it is possible that the North Shoebury site was abandoned before the end of the fourth century. However, Early Saxon pottery found in the material filling the top of the Roman ditches, as well as the

9   North Shoebury Road near the Moat House, looking north.

positioning of an early Saxon cemetery, may indicate that the same field system was still in use in the early fifth century.

Saxons

The Romans were followed by the Saxons, immigrants from Europe, who settled in England from the fifth century. The Saxons established a system of land holdings, based on parishes grouped together in 'Hundreds', which survived the centuries to become the administrative areas of the country. A Hundred denoted an area in which one hundred important men lived.

The area now known as Shoeburyness was divided into two distinct parishes, North Shoebury and South Shoebury, two of the 24 parishes of the Rochford Hundred.

Although there is little evidence of Saxon occupation of North Shoebury, an early Saxon cemetery was discovered (1971) north of St Mary's church, with the bodies arranged in a circle, like the spokes of a wheel. This has been dated to between AD 410-700. Further investigations in 1981 uncovered eight burials and nine cremations. Three of the burials included remains of copper belt buckles, while the cremated remains were found with copper and iron belt fittings, a copper alloy bracelet, fragments of a glass pendant, pottery, part of a bone comb, glass beads and a needlework set. Belt buckles were typical of fifth-century burials, which helps to date these graves as early Saxon. The human remains indicate a family group, including adults and children. It is possible that the cemetery served a small community of Saxon mercenaries and their families who may have been given land in return for military assistance against the Romans. No associated settlement was found in the excavated area.

In 1958, a burial comprising five graves, probably all of adult men, was discovered on the site of the tithe barn on Poynters Lane and is again thought to be early Saxon. A Saxon

10 Bournes Green Chase looking towards Shoebury. On the right is the wall of the White House.

buckle, a pair of scissors and a lead trading token have also been found in Shoebury.

The 1981 excavations produced fragments of at least 24 Saxon pottery vessels, dating to AD 400-600. These wheel-turned pots are comparable with those found in the larger Saxon cemetery at Prittlewell.

Lack of finds that can be dated to the late Saxon period suggests very little human activity in Shoebury at that time (AD 700-1066).

However, the name 'Shoebury' dates from the Saxon period, being based on the Saxon word 'Scoebyrig'. The meaning of 'Shoebury' has been quoted as either 'a fortified position near a shoe shaped piece of land' ('byrig' meaning 'fort')

11 Church Walk, South Shoebury. Before 1950, Shoebury's lanes were lined with elms and hedgerows of black-thorn, hawthorn and wild rose. In spring fields were radiant with buttercups and daisies, glowing with poppies and scabious in summer. Coltsfoot, knapweed, scarlet pimpernel, lady's slipper, chicory, purple orchid and wild garlic grew abundantly.

12   Rectory Lane, with the gate to South Shoebury rectory, 1922.

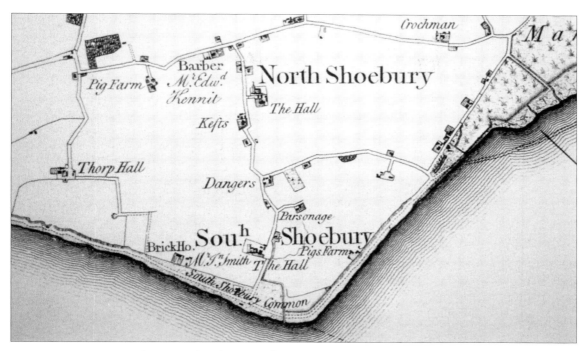

13 Chapman and André's map of 1777, showing North and South Shoebury.

or 'the town in the wood' ('shaw' being the Saxon word for 'wood'). The Saxons also named Wakering 'the settlement of Wacer', Barling 'the settlement of Baerla's people' and Paglesham 'Paeccel's hamlet'. However, the neighbouring manors of Thorpe Hall and Little Thorpe owe their names to the subsequent settlers in the area, the Danes.

Danes and Vikings

From AD 790 Vikings began arriving on the Essex coast. In AD 835 the Danes attacked Sheppey across the Thames estuary from Shoebury, continuing with a series of raids on the south and east coasts of England.

A Danish camp was established at Shoebury, together with another settlement on Foulness. Led by Haesten, the Danes fought the Battle of Benfleet against Alfred the Great in AD 894. Defeated, they fled to their camp at Shoebury where they built defensive ditches and re-

fortified the Iron-Age rampart. Legend says that when Ingvar, one of the Danish leaders, heard of his father's death while at Shoebury, he sat down and gnawed his fingers to the bone with grief. That site is now named after him: Hinguar Street.

Military occupation of the site inhibited extensive archaeological investigation until 1998, and it was only then that the rampart was confirmed as being of Iron-Age, not Danish, origin. As no Danish artefacts were found, it is unlikely that they occupied the site for any length of time.

Soon after they had re-fortified the camp, a raid across to Wales ended with the Danes being driven back to Mersea and the Shoebury camp appears to have been abandoned.

A Danish army was again temporarily based at Shoebury when their king, Canute, successfully fought Edmund Ironside for the English throne at Ashingdon in 1016.

Two

Early Development

From the Saxon period the two parishes, North Shoebury (also called Little Shoebury) comprising some 1,131 acres and South Shoebury (Much Shoebury) with some 1,081 acres, developed as agricultural communities.

During Edward the Confessor's reign (1042-66), both parishes consisted of a single manor (estate) held by one freeman.

When the Norman, William the Conqueror, invaded England in 1066, he claimed all the land as his own and set up his own barons and supporters in charge of the estates. These men became known as 'lords of the manor' and owed allegiance to the king in return for the land. In 1086, William ordered a survey of all the land, tenants and property in England for taxation purposes: the Domesday Survey.

By the time of the survey, North Shoebury parish had been divided into two manors: West Hall (later known as North Shoebury Hall) and Kents (later known as Moated Farm). Each manor had its own tenants who worked the land on behalf of the lord of the manor in return for some land of their own and the lord's protection. Occupation of the parish at this time centred upon a large enclosure south-east of St Mary's church.

The manor of West Hall (Essobiam in the survey) comprised four hides of land (about 480 acres) and was held by the wealthy Norman Suene (sometimes written Sweyne), tenanted for him by a man named Walter. There were four villagers and eight lower-class peasants living on the manor, which included enough woodland to support 12 swine. This wood is thought to have been in the extreme north-west

of the parish. Livestock belonging to the manor included a horse, a pig, six cattle and 115 sheep. Walter owned three ploughs (three teams of eight oxen), while the men owned two ploughs of their own (16 oxen). One of the hides of land was tenanted by one particular freeman and used as pasture for 100 sheep.

The value of West Hall rose from £6 before the Conquest to £8 after it.

The manor of Kents (Soberia in the survey and also known as Sobiam or Little Soiri) was held in demesne (for his own use) by Odo, who was the Bishop of Bayeux and half-brother of William the Conqueror. It comprised one hide (c.120 acres) plus 30 acres of land. Two villagers and three lower-class peasants lived on this manor, with one plough owned between them, plus another two oxen owned by Odo. There was pasture for 40 sheep. This manor was worth 40 shillings before the Conquest and 55 shillings after it. Later, Odo's land was confiscated when he was disgraced, and it is probable that Kents came into Suene's possession.

The single manor in the parish of South Shoebury (like West Hall called Essobiam in the Domesday Survey) was held by Robert Fitzwimarc both before and after the Conquest, when it was passed down to his son Suene. Fitzwimarc was the only pre-Conquest landowner to retain ownership of his lands, because he was a personal friend of William the Conqueror. At Domesday, the manor of South Shoebury is recorded as having five hides of land (c.600 acres), nine villagers and six lower-class peasants. There were two ploughs belonging to Suene and eight ploughs belonging to the

14 North Shoebury Hall, formerly called West Hall.

15 Kents farmhouse, later called Moat House or Moated Farm. It was purchased by George Asser in 1783 and continued in the same ownership as North Shoebury Hall until the 20th century. Samuel Benton Snr rebuilt the house and filled in much of the moat in 1824.

16   South Shoebury Hall, now a listed building of special architectural interest.

villagers, two horses, 16 pigs and 64 sheep. The manor included three acres of meadow and enough woodland to support 20 pigs. By 1086, the value of South Shoebury had risen to £10, from the pre-Conquest value of £6.

From the results of the Domesday Survey, we can estimate that in 1086 the population of North Shoebury, including women and children, was some 60 to 80 people. A similar number lived at South Shoebury. The rising values of the manors show that the area was prospering but, even at this early date, South Shoebury was wealthier, both in terms of land value and the number of livestock, than the combined assets of the two North Shoebury manors.

The parish church buildings, St Andrew's, South Shoebury, and St Mary's, North Shoebury, both date from soon after the Norman Conquest, although they may well replace previous Saxon churches.

The Shoebury manors were eventually inherited by Suene's son, Robert de Essex, who founded Prittlewell Priory in 1100. Around

1165 St Mary's was under the protection of Thomas Becket, Archbishop of Canterbury. However, shortly after his death in 1170, the advowsons (the right to appoint a rector) of both St Mary's and St Andrew's was entrusted to Prittlewell Priory. After the Dissolution of the Priory (1539) the advowson of St Mary's reverted to the Crown and St Andrew's to the lord of the manor.

The parishes were bounded on the west by the parish of Southchurch with Great Wakering parish immediately north of North Shoebury. Both parishes included fields that were described as marsh or saltings, which provided rich grazing land for sheep, a valuable source of meat, wool and milk. Much of the wool was taken by boat to London or Flanders for the weaving trade. The local wool, however, was of coarse quality and in 1343 was fetching four marks per sack less than in other parts of Essex.

The seashore was home to vast numbers of rabbits (introduced by the Normans) and wildfowl. However, the dampness of the marshes, with the associated mist and fogs, meant that malarial fever, known as the ague, was common in the local population.

St Andrew's

South Shoebury parish church, St Andrew's, dates from around 1100-40, being founded by Robert de Essex as an outlier of Prittlewell Priory. Most probably, a monk from the Priory would visit Shoebury to hold services there. The first known incumbent was Peter de Pasinge (1267). The church was situated adjacent to South Shoebury Hall, for the convenience of the lord of the manor, on slightly raised ground overlooking the marshes to the south and east. Before the building boom of the 19th century, the tower was visible from both sides of the ness and served as a landmark for ships.

The fishing activities of the community resulted in the church's dedication to St Andrew, the patron saint of fishermen. A carving representing the mesh of a fishing net and a fish is a feature of the 15th-century timber porch; on either side are shields, one bearing the cross of St Andrew and the other a fish.

Like many South Essex churches, St Andrew's is constructed of rubble, flint and a rough limestone known as ragstone which, in the absence of local building stone, was brought over from Kent.

The first alterations to St Andrew's church were carried out between 1200 and 1250 when recesses were made in the thick walls. The tower was added in the 14th century, also constructed of flint rubble and ragstone, with an internal lining of blocks of chalk. The battlemented brick parapet was added in the 18th century.

In the 15th century, St Andrew's was re-roofed in oak and the wooden porch built. The Norman windows in the nave were replaced at that time with larger ones of the perpendicular style.

17 St Andrew's, South Shoebury, from the north-west corner. Note the empty landscape behind the church on the right.

18   Interior of St Andrew's, South Shoebury, *c.*1905.

fish. Later, the incumbent was resident at The Grove, east of Ness Road. A grove of willows, known as osiers, north of The Grove belonged to South Shoebury Hall and the tenants were required to keep this marshy site stocked with good willow trees.

An early incumbent of one of the Shoebury churches, John de Soberi, was made Dean of Rochford in 1198.

The nave and chancel stonework at St Andrew's was restored in 1852. The vestry was built by voluntary labour in 1902 and in the late 1960s the lath and plaster ceiling was removed to expose the oak beams.

The original rectory was built to the west of St Andrew's church in 1206 and, according to Benton, was a picturesque place with a thatched roof, nooks and crannies and was connected to the church by a pathway. In front of the rectory was a stream known as the Heronry, in which the lord of the manor had a right to hawk and

St Mary's

The present church of St Mary the Virgin dates from *c.*1230 and is believed to be at least the third church built on that site. Like St Andrew's, St Mary's is built mainly of ragstone. The chancel and nave are roofed with handmade clay tiles, but there is evidence of thatch underneath, likely to have been the original

19   St Mary the Virgin, North Shoebury, looking north-east from North Shoebury Road.

roofing material. Its foundations rest on an ancient reed bed.

The chancel is the oldest part of the building, with the nave and south aisle built in the early English style soon afterwards. In 1254, three archways were set into the south wall of the nave, opening to a new south aisle. However, this aisle was demolished in the 14th century and the bays of its arcade filled in. At the same time, the north wall of the nave was rebuilt. The north window of the nave retains fragments of 14th-century glass depicting foliage and borders.

The lower parts of the tower date from the end of the 13th century, while the top stage of the tower was added or rebuilt in the 14th or 15th centuries, with the bell tower the final addition. The pyramid-shaped, weather-boarded tower has a small broach spire. Diagonal buttresses were added to the tower when the north wall of the nave was rebuilt, suggesting that the alterations were to combat instability of the church's foundations.

20 Interior of St Mary the Virgin, North Shoebury, c.1910.

A footpath led from the north-east corner of the churchyard to North Shoebury House on Poynters Lane, but it has not been possible to confirm whether this was once the official rectory. However, from about the 14th century, North Shoebury House and the right to the great tithe payments collected by the

21 Looking north towards St Andrew's church from the Common.

22 View towards Parsons Corner. The fields on the right of this picture were part of White House Farm and now part of the Bishopsteignton Estate.

church was in the hands of tenant farmers, rather than benefiting a rector. Instead, the parish 'made do' with a vicar, who was only entitled to receive the 'small' tithes, and for whom a vicarage was provided further along Poynters Lane, west of Parsons Corner. The field immediately in front of the vicarage belonged to North Shoebury House and the tithe barn, east of Star Lane, was again on North Shoebury House land.

The first recorded rector of North Shoebury is Peter de Hadham who was presented to the living by the Prior of Prittlewell *c.*1250. Another early incumbent was John de Norwich, rector *c.*1350, who went on to become Sub-Dean of Lincoln.

Medieval Shoebury

As might be expected, the farms attached to the manor houses were the largest land holdings in the parish. South Shoebury Hall Farm covered some 300 acres, including a substantial section of the coastline and Shoebury Common. It was the only manor in the parish and, along with the church, was given to Prittlewell Priory by Robert de Essex.

Excavations in South Shoebury indicate a site of medieval settlement east of the Hall, near the site of the garrison church.

West Hall (North Shoebury Hall) farm was of a similar size. The 1981 excavations showed that a large ditched enclosure south-east of St Mary's had been abandoned by 1300 and occupation between 1300-1500 focused on the area of North Shoebury Hall, due south of the church. The medieval field systems continued to influence the settlement patterns of North Shoebury until it was carpeted with housing during the 1980s.

The name West Hall, used at least as early as the reign of Edward IV (1471-83), suggests that the manor house replaced a previous hall further to the east. Excavations revealed medieval and post-medieval pits, gullies and postholes around and under the site of the 16th-century Hall, and 11th- to 12th-century pottery was found there. Medieval pottery was dominated by shell-tempered, locally-made wares. The most common type of 13th-century pot found during the 1981 excavations were cooking vessels with either a flat top or with a turned-down rim above a vertical neck.

Three sides of an early medieval enclosure ditch were found on the farm site immediately east of the Hall. Fields extended nearly continuously from the Hall (roughly the Asda supermarket site), north to Poynters Lane and from the vicarage to North Shoebury House. The arrangement of the fields suggests that strip culture was used in the medieval period.

Early owners of the Hall were Agnes de Shoebury and Henry Gyne. In about 1265 it was purchased by the De Wodeham family of Woodham Ferrers; in 1271, it was held by William de Wodeham, a baron of Rayleigh, who died in 1280. Domestic debris excavated from the site and dated to the 13th century includes the bone remains of a number of suckling pigs, an extravagant form of pig consumption associated with feasting and a high status household. Other remains show that fish, pigs, sheep, cattle, chickens and pheasants were kept. A large quantity of carbonised wheat grain has been attributed to a possible granary fire, with the ruined wheat distributed across the site. Thomas de Wodeham is recorded as owning 140 acres of arable land in North Shoebury in 1328.

In 1328 the Fitz-Simon (Fitz-Symond) family owned Kents and in 1419 purchased West Hall from Edward de Wodeham, along with all the de Wodehams' Shoebury lands.

When Robert Fitz-Symond died in 1472, West Hall descended to Joan Wentworth (neé Fitz-Symond), and it remained in the Wentworth family until at least the mid-16th century. Decorated, high-class pottery dating from the 14th century found on the site of West Hall indicates that the Fitz-Symonds, too, were a wealthy family.

The Fitz-Symonds appear to have sold Kents by 1388, when Richard Kent held 18 acres in Shoebury, although some accounts suggest that Kents was named after a later owner, John Kente.

The Kents estate was mentioned by Norden in his *Speculi Britannica Pars* in 1594 as having a 'house of account'. This house was a long, large building with a double roof standing, as its later name Moated Farm suggests, within a moat just west of North Shoebury Road. Access to the house was via an arch and gate under a building where a drawbridge probably existed.

John Ingoldysbye held Kents during 1466, and after that it belonged to John Kente.

In 1501, the manor of Kents was passed from the trustees of Jasper Tyrell and his wife Margaret to Henry Baker and others. Edward Baker died 3 April 1535, 'Seized of a capital messuage called Kents in Little Shoebury and 100 acres of arable land and 40 acres of pasture'.

The moat at Kents, like that at Suttons, reflects a need for defence during the medieval period.

One of the earliest buildings in South Shoebury was the original Shore House, thought to have been erected during the 12th century of timber gathered from shipwrecks. At low tide, horse-drawn wagons were taken alongside ships anchored offshore and loaded with goods, which were taken back for storage at the Shore House before distribution inland.

23   Gatehouse at Kents. This unusual gatehouse stood over the bridge, possibly a drawbridge, across the moat at Kents.

24   Shore House. The original house was built of ships' timbers as a holding centre to receive goods being landed from ships, prior to their distribution inland.

25   Common and Shore House. A white-tailed eagle was shot on Shoebury common in 1832.

On the surface, both North and South Shoebury parishes were quiet agricultural communities, tucked away in a corner of Essex. However, it was their very location that brought to both Shoeburys a degree of danger and problems unknown to inland parishes. For example, the coastal location put Shoebury in the front line of defence of England and made it a potential target for enemy invasion forces.

Flooding was a regular occurrence, with crops and property often washed away overnight. The sea also brought smugglers and shipwrecks to the area – perhaps seen as a welcome opportunity for some, but for others it meant danger and loss of trade. Marsh fever made the area unhealthy, particularly for newcomers to the area.

Each of the aforementioned problems combined to increase the likelihood of hardship or poverty in the local population.

Richard de Tany held the position of Keeper of the Coast in 1295. He was responsible for all matters relating to the sea and coast of Essex, Suffolk and Norfolk, and had powers to compel people to take part in the defence of the coast. His responsibilities included a network of beacons positioned on high ground near the coast and guarded by the villagers. Shoebury's beacon was said to have been the most important in Essex at this time.

The whole district was on standby in 1305 and again in 1385 from fear of invasion by the French. Landowners John Wodeham and John Fitz-Simond were responsible for rallying a defence force of all able-bodied men. If the alarm was given, they were to assemble on the seashore and light beacons to warn parishes further along the coast.

There was local excitement in 1380 when the Duke of Exeter was trying to escape his enemies via Shoebury. His ship was prevented from sailing by unfavourable winds and he was dragged to shore, from where he was taken to Pleshey and beheaded.

The next year, 1381, the peasants in Kent and Essex rose in protest against taxes and working conditions. John Syrat and John Hart of Shoebury led a local contingent of men who joined the crowd that beheaded tax collectors and clerks on their march to London. Eventually, 500 south Essex men begged for a

26   Ness Road, looking south.

pardon from King Richard and were released on payment of fines. The co-operation between the Kent and Essex peasants during the Peasants' Revolt is further demonstration of the communication links between the two areas. It is likely, with water-borne transport easier and quicker than the rough cart tracks inland, that Shoebury people were more familiar with north Kent than with the north of their own county.

In 1386, an Italian merchant ship ran aground at South Shoebury and the owners claimed that local men had looted 22 bales of pepper and other goods when the crew was forced to take refuge ashore. John Fitz-Simond and John Osborn dealt with the ensuing litigation.

27   Shoebury beach, *c.*1900, with bathing machines and changing tents. One of the first owners of these machines was Sarah Glasscock, wife of Shoebury draper, James.

Three

Tudor and Stuart Shoebury

The Church

The Tudor period was one of unrest for England, as Protestant and Catholic monarchs and their supporters fought to impose their beliefs and doctrines on the population. The church and its ministers exerted enormous influence over the parishioners and parish affairs.

In about 1530 William Stafford, then lord of the manor of Rochford, was appointed to sell off local church bells to raise money in the area and, in Shoebury, St Andrew's bells were among those sold. The money from the Foulness bells was used to repair the sea walls, but it is not known what happened to the money from St Andrew's. However, the bells were eventually replaced.

In 1537, Henry VIII granted ownership of South Shoebury manor to Sir Richard Rich of Rochford Hall, a land-grabbing opportunist, in 2006 voted by the BBC *History Magazine* as the 'villain of the century' for the 1500s. In 1539 he let the manor to William Friend for 30 years at a rent of £40 p.a.

The Rev. Richard Byworthy was deprived of the North Shoebury living in 1554 for being married. His vocation proved more valued than his marriage as he separated from his wife, did penance and was restored to the church.

At the accession of Elizabeth I (1558) a proclamation was issued that people were to restrain themselves from believing any doctrine except the gospels, epistles and Ten Commandments. Thomas Pike, who owned land in North Shoebury, eager to act upon this edict, went into St Mary's and pulled down the

statues and paintings. However, this was not universally popular and Pike was taken before Lord Rich who was instructed to punish him according to his offence, i.e. that he had been too fast and zealous before Parliament had had time to consult fully on the proclamation. There is no record of Pike's punishment and Philip Benton suggests that Lord Rich, who had Puritan sympathies, probably prevaricated until Pike was forgotten.

A namesake of his, Arthur Pyke of North Shoebury, had more mundane problems to deal with when in 1576 he found himself bailed by Robert Prentice of Barling. Pyke's offence was to hide his servant Jerome Davenyshe after a warrant had been sent for his arrest. Pyke was ordered by the General Sessions court either to bring forth the servant or to pay the North Shoebury churchwardens 8d. a week towards

28 St Andrew's from the south. Note how the ivy nearly covers the church tower. Carving on the 15th-century porch depicts a fishing net and fish.

29   St Mary's Church, from the north-west corner with North Shoebury Hall behind. The large tomb to the left of this picture belongs to Philip Benton's parents.

the bringing up of 'a bastard child begotten by the said Jerome in North Shoebury'. Pyke may have wished that he had turned the servant in immediately because the next year, 1577, Pyke found himself bailed again and similarly charged either to present Jerome Davenyshe to the court or to pay 8d. weekly to the churchwardens of Dunton 'for the upkeep of a bastard child begotten by the said Jerome at Dunton'.

Perhaps Davenyshe would have fared better with more of an example set by the local clergy. In 1565(6?), the wife of Robert Hawks, vicar of North Shoebury, was accused of committing adultery with local man William Stevens. In South Shoebury the rector Thomas Martyndall (1562-7) was 'a dicer and a carder' and one Christmas lost all of £3.

The monarch again influenced local life when in January 1591 Elizabeth I gave North Shoebury House and the advowson of the church to Henry Best and John Welles.

One of the best known rectors of South Shoebury is Cambridge graduate, the Rev. Arthur Dent. During his incumbency (1580-1602) he published several puritanical sermons, written 'especially for the comfort of Protestants and the daunting of Papists, Seminary priests and all that cursed rabble'. However, it was his book *The Plaine Man's Pathway to Heaven* that brought Dent the most fame. The book was specifically targeted at 'the ignorant and vulgar sort' to encourage morality as well as religion and described a man's journey from this world to the next. The book ran to 24 editions and was used as a model for John Bunyan's *Pilgrims' Progress*.

Despite his own education, Dent demonstrated his empathy with his simple parishioners when he admonished a visiting preacher for an overly-intellectual sermon. He showed the visitor pitchforks, hoes and other tools for sale near the church and asked what he would think if

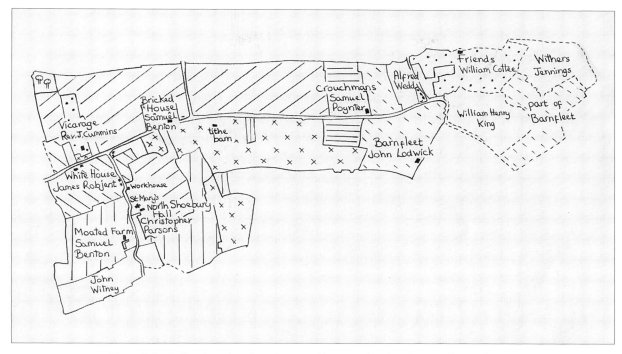

30 Map of North Shoebury based on the 1839 tithe map, showing farms and occupiers.

31 Map of South Shoebury based on the 1848 tithe map, showing farms and occupiers.

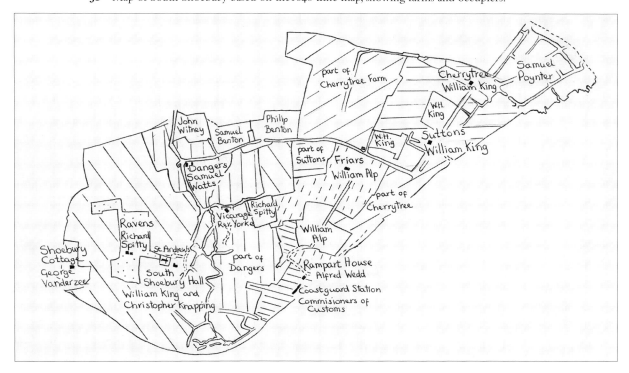

32   The Avenue, 1907. An 18th-century writer described Shoebury as having 'narrow lanes where the rooks built in the large trees'.

London merchants came down to sell diamonds or silver. The preacher thought that would be ridiculous. 'Just so with your Cambridge-ware,' said Dent. 'The next time you come to my parish, bring shovels and spades and plain truths.'

Although Robert Rich had granted him the living of South Shoebury, Dent was offended when Rich's domestic chaplain at Rochford Hall, Robert Wright, referred to the local clergy as 'a pack of dumb dogs'. Dent joined with priests from Rochford, Leigh, Southchurch, Shopland and Prittlewell against Wright, and petitioned the Secretary of State to have him removed, giving Wright's rejection of the Book of Common Prayer as the reason. Wright was briefly imprisoned.

Dent himself fell out of favour with the Bishop when he refused to wear a surplice or make the sign of the cross at baptism, both of which were deemed compulsory under

Elizabeth I's Book of Common Prayer. Dent died of a fever in 1602.

The Rev. Edward Lane (1605-85) also found recognition as a theological writer.

One local man of God who was apparently not so popular was the Rev. William Hayward and the courts heard in 1588 that John Bridge of North Shoebury 'did lay violent hands on the minister'. However, records do not reveal the reason or the outcome.

The poverty of some at this time can be judged from some of the cases that were brought to court. In 1632, for example, Thomas Earle and William Osborne of North Shoebury broke into the house of Dorothy Raymond one night and stole 'four bushells of wheaten meale worth 10s'. Earle was found not guilty but Osborne was found guilty and died in jail before his sentence was passed.

One of the duties of the archdeacon, or his officials, was to visit the churches in his diocese to check up on the vicar and his upkeep of the church. It appears that St Mary's warranted these visits for in 1574 the chancel was found to be 'in great decay' and, in 1618, there was a reprimand for Richard Holman 'For not repayring the chauncell being p'son [parson] of the same'. Similarly, in 1630, the archdeacon's court held at Great Baddow recorded that St Mary's 'chancell lyeth uncovered with the glass windows broken, so that the parishioners cannot sitt drye, neither at service nor at the Communion table'. Perhaps there were no glaziers available in Shoebury, as the parish's answer to the problem of broken windows was to have them blocked up. However, in 1684 another visitation ordered that 'the windows that are mortared up in ye Chancell to be beaten out and glazed'.

When St Andrew's was inspected in 1611, Samuel Ffrend and John Kinge were admonished for neglecting the leading and shingling.

Communications

Despite its long coastline, the sandbanks and gradient of the shore at Shoebury meant there was no deep-water inlet suitable for shipbuilding. A report on Essex made January 1564-5 showed that North and South Shoebury, between them, had one vessel, one master and owner, and four mariners and fishermen. In contrast, Barling had 23 vessels, 15 masters and 48 mariners and fishermen; Prittlewell had 10 vessels, 15 masters and 36 mariners and fishermen. Therefore, it seems that the residents of Shoebury continued to be primarily concerned with agriculture.

John Norden's map of 1594 depicts only two roads into and out of South Shoebury: one route running due west from St Andrew's, and a second road from St Andrew's leading north-east, across the sands to Foulness Church. This latter road is described in the *Essex Review* of 1927 thus:

The way goes curving eastwards for a mile from Wakering Stairs … until it is nearly half that distance from the shore, and then turns north-eastwards to keep almost straight ahead for the next five miles … Between three and four hundred broom-like plants are now maintained as guiding marks on the seaward side of the main track, and give it the local title of the Broomway.

The 1622 edition of Camden's *Britannia* shows a circular road passing through Shoebury, Southend, Rochford and Great Wakering.

It was probably the poor state of the roads that caused a tragic accident on 30 April 1592 when local boy William Cerb, just eight years old, was driving a cart pulled by two horses. His cargo was a maypole, no doubt part of the preparations for the May Day celebrations the next day, an annual event much enjoyed by the local children. William's cart overturned and fell on him, part of it piercing the nape of his neck, killing him instantly. The inquest noted that the horses belonged to William Bridge of North Shoebury and were worth 40s. each; the cart belonged to Richard Hull of Great Wakering.

Property

South Shoebury Hall, originally thatched, was rebuilt in 1568 with a timber frame and

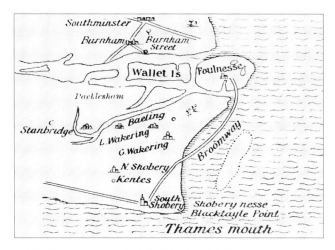

33 Based on a map by John Norden, this illustration shows the roads to Shoebury, *c.*1594. The Broomway was only passable at low tide.

34   North Shoebury Hall, *c.*1915, seen from North Shoebury Road. The house was entirely rebuilt by John Gregory Welch in 1797.

weatherboarding. The entrance hall floor was laid with cobblestones brought from Holland as ballast in a sailing barge.

North Shoebury Hall too was completely rebuilt during the 16th century as a Tudor brick hall with weatherboarding to the upper storey. Remains of its foundations include several pieces of worked stone, which may have been brought to the site from elsewhere but, most likely, came from the demolished south aisle of St Mary's.

Cherrytree Farm dates from 1568 and Barnfleet from 1584.

When Suttons (Sutton Hall) was rebuilt in 1681, it took the title Shoebury Manor and became the preferred residence of the lord of the manor. Since that date, the manorial courts, dealing with local crimes and property transfers, were held there rather than at South Shoebury Hall, leading to Suttons being locally referred to as 'the manor house', although the court was transferred back to South Shoebury Hall in 1800. Tenants were obliged to attend the courts. However, the mundane proceedings were usually accompanied by a sumptuous meal.

Suttons, its lawn, flower garden and red brick wall, was surrounded by a moat crossed by two bridges from the road and another towards the common and shore. The hall and drawing rooms either side of it were panelled in oak. At the rear of the ground floor were a study, an office and the servants' rooms: kitchen, scullery, larder, storerooms. There were four bedrooms on the first floor, five on the second floor and two servants' attic rooms above that. In addition, the house had a basement and extensive cellars.

The grounds of Suttons included a stable block and coach yard as well as an orchard with apricot, peach and fig trees. The house was known as Kennets or Kings during the residence of families by those names. The common in front of Suttons was the site of an early tide mill.

Ownership passed through Lord Rich's descendants, the Earls of Warwick, until sold in the 17th century to Daniel Finch, Earl of Nottingham. As lord of the manor in 1673, the earl was ordered to carry out an inspection of

35   Suttons, South Shoebury, built in 1681, was once known as Kennets and later as Kings. The water in the foreground of this picture is part of the moat that originally surrounded the house. Suttons has been occupied by the military since 1889 when the New Ranges was formed.

the Essex coast to determine the likelihood of an enemy landing. He travelled along the coast accompanied by the gentlemen of the locality and concluded that, as the countryside had 'very strong ditches and hedges', there was very little danger of invasion and any attacks were likely to be concentrated at Leigh or Milton (south of Prittlewell).

The coastal location involved the parishes in dealing with bodies washed ashore from shipwrecks or swept overboard from passing ships during storms. Several sailors perished on the flats off Shoebury and inquests into these drownings were held at the Halfway House, so named for being halfway between Shoebury and Southend. Often, it fell to South Shoebury parish ratepayers to withstand the cost of funeral expenses, as the parish overseers' accounts record, for example: 'for burying a man on the beach at South Shoebury 1s 6d'.

In 1673 the Earl built the Red Brick House at the junction of what is now Elm Road and Wakering Road, as a lodge for Suttons manor house. Visitors had to pass through the Red

House gate and along 'a beautiful avenue lined with trees that formed an archway overhead'. A brick panel on the south gable bears the letters FR with the letter M above it, two hearts and the date 1673. The same insignia was on Suttons' weather vane, with the date 1681. The initials are thought to refer to the builder Francis Haydaston and his wife Rebecca, although she died in 1639. Several windows were bricked up

36   Red Brick House (Old Red House), Wakering Road. Originally built as a gatekeeper's lodge at the end of the drive to Suttons, the south-facing gable bears the initials M and Fr, two hearts and the date 1673.

37   Another view of Red Brick House. The notice on the conservatory advertises 'cauliflowers for sale'.

during the 17th century to avoid window tax. The Red House later accommodated Suttons' gardener and steward.

The Earl sold most of his Shoebury estates to the Bristow family, who had returned from America in 1680.

38   The vicarage, North Shoebury, viewed from Bournes Green Chase. The house was rebuilt by the Rev. Henry Wilmot in 1884.

In 1659, the rectory and church of North Shoebury was sequestered and leased to Robert Roane of Surrey for £35 10s. For this payment, Roane was entitled to collect the annual tithes which, before they were converted into a monetary payment in about 1840, were made up of wheat, rye, barley, peas, beans and oats. This arrangement left only the small tithes for the vicar who possibly, therefore, could not depend on North Shoebury for his whole income resulting in pluralism. For example, Gabriel Price, rector of Ashingdon in 1621, was also vicar of North Shoebury. In cases like this, one of the parishes was often left in the charge of an even more poorly paid and inexperienced curate.

Historian William King excuses this sequestration of the living as it was of such small value. However, Philip Benton felt both North and South Shoebury had been badly treated, saying: 'With respect to the clergy, it

39 Poynters Lane, looking east towards North Shoebury House. The road was named after Samuel Poynter, tenant of Crouchmans Farm 1833-86 and North Shoebury churchwarden for many years. Crouchmans farmhouse was completely rebuilt after a fire on 11 July 1864.

is notorious that for the majority of more than two centuries, they were noted for their incompetence, their vices and shameful neglect of their duties.'

Arthur Trevor, the owner of North Shoebury House, was obviously more concerned for his own pocket than the spiritual well-being of the residents of North Shoebury and, in 1663, the rectory and church was leased for 17 years at £36 p.a. to local widow Ann Dates (Daly?). The rent was payable at the cheesemonger's shop of William Davy in Thames Street, London. No doubt this was convenient for Arthur Trevor.

By 1680 ownership of North Shoebury House had come to John Chetwynd of Middlesex, and he continued the tradition of renting it out, this time to another local widow, Katherine Goodlad. Katherine paid £97 4s. 4d. p.a. for 21 years, the property including 150 acres of

land, several fields of which bore interesting names such as Jollyfaxes, Moor Joyes, Morits and Rowleys (all spelt slightly differently in successive leases). In addition, the lease required Katherine to provide 'two fat cock turkeys and two capons and six bushells of apples upon the five and twentieth day of December yearly'. She was also obliged to provide 'free entertainment, dyet and lodging' for Chetwynd, his friends, servants and horses for three days and nights every year, to enable him to visit the property and ensure it was being properly managed. Part of this management included an agreement to plant 20 young trees of elm, oak or ash, plus six crabapple trees near the house every year. The lessee was responsible for the repairs to both the house and the church, although Chetwynd was quick to minimise his own responsibilities by specifying in the lease that '… the old Barn

40   Coastguard station, built on Beacon Field in 1825. It was almost completely rebuilt by the military, with just a minute portion of the original building remaining.

that stands in the field called the seven acres is not intended to be continued in repairs'.

National Defence

Shoebury was still considered a strategic defence point of the Thames estuary and, in April 1619, it was certified that there were five official beacons in the Rochford Hundred: 'Foullnes, Canuden, Shoberry, Milton and Rayley' – the most of any Hundred in Essex. Local men were trained to prepare the beacons with materials for burning and for watching the beacons. However, any comfort from this early warning defence system must have been offset by the need to raise local taxes to cover the costs of fuel, repairs and watching. On 28 April 1619 it was decreed that it was no longer necessary to watch the beacons.

When Charles I (1625-49) demanded money for ship building in 1634, 17 people in North Shoebury and 18 people in South Shoebury were assessed, and the parishes had to provide £6 10s and £6 respectively.

During the Civil War (1642-51) most of the Rochford Hundred was sympathetic to the Puritan cause, the lower classes being much influenced by local priests. The Earls of Warwick had Puritan sympathies and held the right of presentation to the livings of South Shoebury as well as Hadleigh, Leigh, Ashingdon, Prittlewell, Rochford, Foulness, Hawkwell, Southchurch and Shopland.

41 The cliffs at South Shoebury. Local residents complained that horses exercising on the beach were jumping over breakwaters, frightening and endangering children and adults.

In 1666, during the second Dutch Wars, the Dutch anchored at Gun Fleet off Shoebury after four days' battle at sea and the district was put on alert. The English fleet collected at the Nore, a sandbank in the estuary, with a fleet of about 90 ships, matching the Dutch. When the winds were favourable, they engaged the Dutch and defeated them.

When a Dutch invasion was feared during 1667, a brigade of the Essex Militia was deployed from Hadleigh to Shoebury and beacons were again lit to warn the district to prepare. The English fleet was again anchored off Shoebury and the Dutch Vice-Admiral's ship was grounded nearby. Trinity House asked for assistance from the naval authorities to set the Shoebury beacon for the better security of warships and for licences to prevent the men in charge of the beacon from being pressed into naval service.

No doubt the residents of Shoebury were hoping for a quieter life in the following century.

Four
Community Spirit 1700-1800

❖

Despite its national importance in the defence of the realm, both North and South Shoebury continued as agricultural communities where most of the population were poor farm workers.

Before the days of national census, population counts were often the responsibility of the clergy. In 1723 South Shoebury was thought to be home to only 25 individuals, although by 1763 this estimate had risen to 69, and that of North Shoebury was 115.

Administrative Affairs

On a daily basis the parishes were concerned with the care of their poorer neighbours, the upkeep of the local roads and punishment of offenders. From Tudor times, these issues were dealt with by the parish 'vestry', a committee of local men (rarely women) consisting of churchwardens, surveyors, overseers and constables.

The Highway Surveyors were responsible for ensuring that every landowner in the parish

42 Church Road, South Shoebury. This road, like St Andrew's Road, was made up as far as Richmond Avenue in 1902. It was more than 30 years before it was extended to Maplin Way.

43   Pond, Ness Road. Farmers brought their cattle to drink at this pond next to the Well House. The Well House was given to the Poor of South Shoebury parish, the rent from it supplementing the poor relief rates.

spent an appropriate number of days each year maintaining the public roads. However, court records show that many people tried to shirk these responsibilities. In July 1650, for example, John Canon and Richard Harding of South Shoebury jointly owned 80 acres of land in Great Wakering but had not worked on the roads at all that year. Similarly, Jeremy Cranwell of North Shoebury owned 50 acres of land but did no work on the roads. The surveyors requested that, unless these men performed the requisite amount of work within the next six weeks, they be fined appropriately.

The Overseers of the Poor collected tax from all landowners to be put towards the support of the poor, sick, widowed and orphans of the parish. As this support came directly out of their pockets, parishioners were keen to ensure that

they were only paying for those entitled to their support. Robert Peach and his family fell foul of this system when, suffering hard times in 1652, they rented a house in Little Wakering. The Little Wakering constables obtained a warrant and removed the family and all their possessions back to South Shoebury, where they had previously been living. The constables of South Shoebury, in return, applied to the courts for permission to convey Peach, his wife and children back to Little Wakering. It is cases like this that led to the formal Act of Settlement in 1662, which restricted the movement of anyone who did not own freehold land.

In 1733, two orphaned boys were taken in by Richard Kennet and Samuel Oakley, for which they were paid £2 a week by the parish. Unemployed adults would be paid a weekly

44   The Pyghtle Cottage, North Shoebury Road. The cottage stood between the church and the workhouse and was used as a weaving cottage by the inmates. Subsequently, it was the home of the May family for about 100 years. It became dilapidated and was pulled down in about 1989.

sum in addition to having their rent paid. They could also apply for one-off payments for specific items For example, in April 1733, the overseers 'bought a bed and a bath and a blankit and ould quilt for Smith'.

The 1723 Workhouse Act enabled parishes to provide communal workhouses, rather than supporting the poor in their own homes or lodgings. North and South Shoebury and Foulness parishes joined together to rent a building called High House, just north of St Mary's, for use as a workhouse.

Monthly parish meetings were held at the workhouse, with absent officers being fined 10 shillings. The wealthier Foulness parish contributed 40 shillings to the meeting while North and South Shoebury paid 25 shillings each. This money provided dinner for the parish officers including, records indicate,

an ample quantity of punch. As coal was expensive at 29 shillings per cauldron, bean straw, 7s. 6d. per load, was used to heat the workhouse.

Between the workhouse and St Mary's stood the Pyghtle (pronounced Pikle, a Celtic word for a parcel of land), a cottage and garden. This cottage was used as a weaving room where workhouse inmates would spin worsted. Wool was brought from Suffolk in a state called 'locks'; it was then spun and reeled and sold to be dyed and to supply the manufacturers of 'bays and says'. About 1800, the spinning wheels cost 3s. 6d. each and spindles 9d. per half dozen. The receipts for spinning were about £14 per year.

A workhouse governor and sub-governor were employed, while the inmates had to wear the letter P and the first letter of their parish on their right shoulder. The workhouse furniture, worth about £100, was all sold around 1830 under the Rev. Commins.

Other outgoings from the parish coffers involved sick payments. In 1766, smallpox cases were heavy and accounts record several payments for sick families. The workhouse was also used as a repository for sick people.

The Rev. William Phillips, curate of St Andrew's and later vicar of St Mary's (1774-89), was a qualified doctor and completed the registers with clear, precise handwriting, detailing his parishioners' cause of death. For example, St Mary's registers for 1777 show: Richard Kennett 0 whooping cough; Robert Kennett 37 fever; Mary Harpum 32 childbed; George Hauce 74 decay.

However, Phillips offended other members of the clergy when he published a sermon entitled *Clerical Misconduct Reprobated*.

Particularly severe floods were recorded in 1099, 1236, 1376 and 1552. James Ramsey, rector of South Shoebury, noted in February 1705 that 'a very extraordinary tide overflowed the banks and in several places made large breaches that this parish and many places more suffered greatly by the inundation'. Benton mentions another flood in 1735 when 'this parish suffered greatly'.

Even without flooding, the shore remained a treacherous place and the rector of St Andrew's, Luke Imber (1727-73), recorded the following story in the parish registers 12 March 1741:

45 View from North Shoebury Road across the pond to St Mary's. In 1931, North Shoebury was described as 'a charming cluster of farms'.

Be it a warning ever hereafter. This evening Wiggins a hoyman brought in his vessel from London the Rev. Mr Silke, and set him by help of his little boat on ye sands call'd West Knock Sands which are two miles distant from shoar. The gentleman was a stranger and 'twas dark and 'tis believed he perish'd in the swimms or creeks, the tide flowing before he could reach shoar and if ye tide did not flow 'tis scarce possible for a stranger to come safe ashore.

The name 'knock' is from knoll, a hillock. Four other sandbanks off Shoebury were known hitherto as 'the Shoobery, Blacktail, the Shoo and the Whittaker', and the *Maritime Atlas* of 1740 refers to 'This sand that beareth these four appellations ... now known as the Maplin'. Thus, sometime early in the 18th century, these sands received the name of the Maplins or the Maplin Sands.

The Rev. Imber contributes much to the history of Shoebury by his careful notes in the parish registers and warned that it was not only strangers who were in danger from the tides with the following tale. In November 1761, a Foulness fisherman, 20-year-old Henry Hockett, 'was driven ashore in this parish [South Shoebury]. He tumbled overboard from his own boat about a fortnight since, was much eaten by the fish and was known by his book of accounts found in his pocket.'

The registers for 1764 show that others have only themselves to blame for their demise: 'John Dimond, a reputed good fidler, had drank too freely and fell into a ditch by the roadside from whence he had scrambled out, but ye weather very cold and he wet, tis believed he perishe'd by those means ...'. A verdict of accidental death was recorded.

In 1749 St Andrew's benefited from new seats and rails and from 'beautification' by courtesy of money from the sale of two cracked bells. Eleven years later, the Rev. Imber noted in the registers: '... every part of the Chancel of South Shoebury within and without was finished ... at the sole expense of L. Imber the Rector ... note that ye door and ye rails at ye communion table are a free gift to ye parishioners who are obliged at all times to keep such in repair.'

Present and future incumbents of St Andrew's will be pleased to note that Thomas Evans, the carpenter who carried out the work, added the following: 'Note that the parishioners very willingly offered to do their parts as to the communion rails, table and floor but the boarding of ye floor being a new thing the rector did it at his expense and this is to be remembered hereafter to be no precedent for future rectors.'

The parsonage barn had been entirely rebuilt by the previous rector, Robert Drew (1715-27), who had also spent £136 repairing and rebuilding the rectory. However, the Rev. Imber noted that 'no stable was found on the parsonage and an entire new stable was erected at ye expense of ye Rector'.

Horses would have been essential for a country rector who wished to visit his parishioners – not only were they the only transport available but they were ideally suited to the rutted cart tracks and by-ways that served as roads in the Shoebury area.

Peter Lodwick, owner of Crouchmans Farm (named after 15th-century owner John Croucheman), married Elizabeth Kennet (widow of Robert Kennet) by licence in St Mary's on 28 August 1759. The Rev. Imber recorded that a register had 'been often requested by the minister' but 'the officers have neglected to buy' and he had had to borrow the South Shoebury register to make the required entry. The marriage was also notable as the couple rode to the church together on one horse, Elizabeth riding pillion behind her fiancé.

It has been said that the Rev. Imber wed a 13-year-old girl in 1762, when he himself was eighty. He died in October 1773 at the age of ninety-one.

46   South Shoebury rectory, 1915.

47   Old Red House at the junction of High Street, Elm Road, Wakering Road and Blackgate Road. The signpost directs people to Southend, Great Wakering, New Ranges, Barracks and Railway Station.

48   East Beach. One of the more colourful characters of the village was fisherman Joseph Cundy (1814-94), who lived in an up-turned boat on East Beach.

Fishing

Farming continued as the main occupation in the parish throughout the 18th century, most men being employed as agricultural labourers. Hay and straw from the local farms was sent to London, partly by road and partly by barge. However, some made their livings from fishing. Daniel Defoe wrote in 1722 that from the flats off Shoebury to the mouth of Colne Water:

> ... the shoar is full of shoals and sands, with some deep channels between; all which are so full of fish that not only the Barking fishing-smacks come hither to fish, but the whole shoar is full of small fisher-boats, in very great numbers, belonging to the villages and towns on the coast, who come in every tide with what they take, and, selling the smaller fish in the country, send the best and largest away upon horses which go night and day to London market ...

The chief fish were sole, 'sometimes exceedingly large', which fetched a good price at market. In addition, turbot, whiting, codling and large flounders were a common catch.

Mr Outing of Southchurch is credited with being the first to undertake the cultivation of oysters on the south Essex shore. In 1791 it was noted that Shoebury was famous for large quantities of oysters sent to the London markets, as well as an immense number of mussels and cockles.

There had been several disputes over the fishing rights off the coast of Southchurch, Thorpe Hall and South Shoebury and in 1738 a court case was held to define legally the extent of the rights of each of these manors.

Smuggling and wrecking

Philip Benton wrote of the Rochford Hundred: 'The whole district is honeycombed with

49   View looking south to the Shore House, which had a defensive trapdoor across the top of the stairs.

traditions concerning smuggling …'. This lucrative yet dangerous trade offered much incentive to poor agricultural labourers or fishermen and Shoebury men were no doubt as involved as any.

Although the sandbanks off Shoebury inhibited the rapid and furtive slipping ashore practised by smugglers at Paglesham and Leigh, the design of several Shoebury buildings suggests that the locals co-operated in the illicit trade. At Suttons, for example, the large cellars are thought to have been used to stash kegs of gin and other booty throughout the 18th century, while a tunnel led from the cellars to the seashore, and another to the Red Brick House.

Cherrytree Farm, originally built in 1568 north of Suttons, was rebuilt in 1678 of red brick, with a massive oak staircase and a trap door that could be lowered over the top of the stairs.

The Shore House, too, had a defensive trapdoor secured by bolts over the stairs, suggesting that the residents felt in need of protection and secrecy. Gaps in the platform allowed 'unwelcome visitors' to be further deterred with gunfire.

Benton also refers to 'an old solitary barn used for smuggling purposes' on Rampart Farm.

One incident from the 1760s tells how customs officials at Leigh boarded a smuggling vessel but were attacked and held prisoner until high tide. The boat made its way to Shoebury Ness where a party of horsemen was waiting on the beach. The goods, 50 oilskin bags of tea and small barrels of brandy, were spirited away into the Shoebury countryside.

Mrs W. Knapping, writing in the 1890s, retold stories of the many respectable Shoebury farmers who would be quite unperturbed to find their wagons and horses requisitioned during the night, and a corresponding gift of a keg or two of brandy secreted in their stable. Such practices were common until the 1840s.

When there was a strong north wind, local fishermen would moor on the Maplin Sands for a few days, showing a light in their top rigging at night. These lights were often the cause of cargo or merchant ships going ashore on the sands. Assistance was then offered by the fishermen who rowed through the shallow water to the stranded vessel and helped to refloat her. Not only could they secure money from the ships' captains for this assistance but could appropriate cargo thrown overboard to lighten the load.

50 Star House, Poynters Lane, c.1940. This cottage on the corner of Star Lane was licensed as a public house from 1769-84. A black dog, a portent of bad luck, was said to haunt Star Lane.

However, officially, all goods washed up onto the shore became the property of the lord of the manor, as Abraham Wells found to his cost in 1763. The Court held at North Shoebury Hall heard that when a cask of strong beer (porter) was cast up, Wells 'carried away said butt and porter for his own use'. He was summoned to the court where he admitted his crime and was ordered to hand over the butt and pay £1 15s. fine.

In 1760, a coast waiter was appointed to South Shoebury, taking responsibility for any goods landed on the beach. In addition, Shoebury was the base for a riding officer whose duty was to patrol the coast between Leigh and Wakering to foil smuggling plans.

In 1797 the Nore fleet hoisted the red flag and blockaded the Thames, refusing passage to all ships, in protest at the conditions seamen worked under. As provisions ran low on the ships, local fishermen did a flourishing trade in food with the mutineers.

Village life

It is probable that the licensees of the local alehouse were delightedly complicit in the smuggling trade. Star House was built with a large cellar in 1753 on the corner of Poynters Lane and Star Lane, North Shoebury and was licensed as an alehouse as early as 1769 when its licensee was George Chaplin. John and Jane Brooks took over the licence in 1770, followed by James Benewith from 1773 to 1776. The Star then came under the care of William Foot who retained the licence until 1784, when the building reverted to a labourer's cottage. Star House was demolished in about 1950.

One local who more than likely regretted the demise of the Star was the Rev. Thomas Archer (1750-1832), curate of South Shoebury, who was well known for his love of the good things in life. From Eton and Cambridge, his career took him from North Benfleet to Prittlewell and then Southchurch, where he was also responsible for South Shoebury. No doubt his religious responsibilities were dutifully carried out, but Archer did not let that curtail his pleasures. During the hunting season, for example, he wore his scarlet beneath his surplice and immediately after the service would collect his hunter from the church gate and ride to the hunt. Once, when conducting a marriage, the hunt passed the church and Archer shouted out 'Tally ho! Tally ho!'. If he had any appointment, he would start walking down the aisle during the last prayer, taking his surplice off at the same time. Benton described him as an 'eccentric and singular man' who usually wore a blue frock coat, white corduroys and grey worsted stockings without gaiters.

Thomas Archer died at Foulness in February 1832 aged 82 and his epitaph remembers him as 'a friend to the poor'.

A less popular member of the clergy about this time was the Rev. John C, curate of both North and South Shoebury, who was sent the following suggestion for an epitaph by a dissatisfied parishioner:

A soldier, pastor both in one
Lies beneath this honoured stone.
He never fought, he never taught,
No doubt to Heaven, his soul is gone.
And since to us he never came
The good to praise, or bad reclaim,
To kiss our wives, or raise our tithes,
We pay this tribute to his name.

However, Shoebury was not exclusive in this respect and during the 17th and 18th centuries there was thought to be only about five vicars/rectors who were resident in their parishes in the whole of the Rochford Hundred, while curates were given responsibility for four or five churches each. James Ramsay (1675-1715), for example, was also the vicar of Great Wakering and allowed South Shoebury rectory to become 'ruinous'. The living at North Shoebury was, however, augmented by £200 of Queen Anne's Bounty and £200 given by Bishop Robinson in 1719.

From the 18th century, the highest status members of the community were no longer the landowners themselves, as most of the farms were under the management of tenant farmers. The owners were typically London residents. For example, North Shoebury Hall had been rented to tenant farmers from at least 1664 when it was in the possession of John Cage of Maidstone.

In 1722, George Asser of Southchurch purchased West Hall (North Shoebury Hall) and land in North and South Shoebury. Although the Assers were relatively local, their Shoebury lands continued to be rented to farmers, including North Shoebury Hall Farm, which was leased to Christopher Parsons from 1739. Far from the suckling pigs found during the medieval period, cheap tin-glazed earthenware pottery dating from the mid-18th century found on the site indicates that this was not a wealthy household at that time.

The shops and lands at North Shoebury junction were known as Stocks Pieces, from the location of the village stocks. Its oldest known owner is Benjamin Hawkins of 'Pricklewell' a cordweyner (shoemaker) who sold the house, orchard and two acres of land in 1679 to William Hogg, a tanner from Barking. In 1776 it was sold to Christopher Parsons together with Palgraves in Southchurch for £1,075. The property remained in the Parsons family for several generations and became known as Parson's Corner.

In 1764, when Thomas Drew and Frances Asser, the then lord and lady of the manor, heard that there were no stocks within the jurisdiction

51 Parsons Corner, the centre of North Shoebury, is named after the Parsons family who owned this land and property from 1776 to 1882. On the left is the blacksmith's house. The stocks stood in the centre of the crossroads.

52 Shoebury Cross House, an 18th-century weather-boarded cottage, served as the post office and only shop in North Shoebury for centuries. In 1887 all these buildings, plus gardens and outbuildings, were purchased for £590.

53   Danger Farm (formerly Dawes and later called Cooks Farm) at the junction of Elm Road and Ness Road was demolished on 16 May 1906. In 1534, Edward Barber held fights here.

of North Shoebury, they ordered that stocks be immediately erected 'in the usual place'. Petty criminals would have been sentenced to the stocks at the local courts held at North Shoebury Hall. Those committing more serious crimes would have been transported to the Quarter Session courts held at Chelmsford.

In 1763 Parsons undertook to reconstruct an old barn on North Shoebury Hall Farm. He paid the builders £57, including £1 for taking down the old barn and selling the timbers that were too old for re-use for use as laths. The construction was a lengthy process and Mr Bowes, the carpenter, had to cut and saw new timber in November, leaving it to season for two months but, despite his care, had to wait nearly a year for his payment. The finished barn had three sections: an entrance porch, storage

for hay and a granary. The doors were large enough for a loaded cart to pass through. The barn was in service for nearly 200 years and transformed into a public house in the 1980s.

In 1761, the rateable value of North Shoebury was £549, slightly more than the £533 that South Shoebury was worth. However, in contrast, Foulness was rated at £2,545.

The end of the 18th century saw much improvement of the buildings in both North and South Shoebury, suggesting an era of prosperity for the local farmers. For example, Thomas Parsons extended South Shoebury Hall in 1766, adding a brick-built, four-room extension behind the original house plus two attics. A round outbuilding was (it is thought) used for bee-keeping.

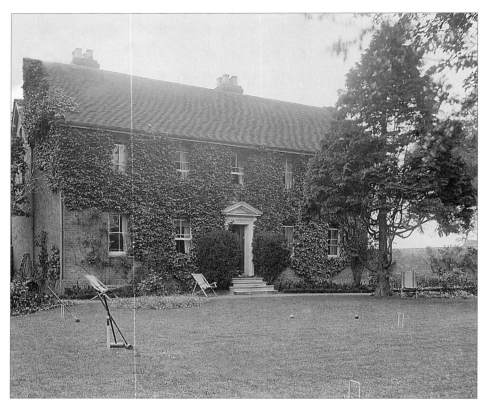

54 The White House, Bournes Green Chase, dates from at least 1330 and was at one time called Barbours after early owner Peter Barber. The original house had decorative plasterwork and ornamental windows. It was purchased by Robert Kennet in 1732 and rebuilt in yellow brick by Edward Kennet in 1787. It is now a listed building.

In 1781, the house at Danger Hall Farm (also called Dawes and later Cooks) was rebuilt at the junction of Ness Road and Elm Road. It was one of the largest farms in the parish with fields stretching from the boundary with North Shoebury almost to the estuary coast.

55   Friars farmhouse was built in the High Street in 1796 and demolished in 1974.

Doors Farm, named after tenant Daniel Door (1730-68), straddled the boundary of North and South Shoebury and was also completely rebuilt in 1781. The house, tradition states, was formerly inhabited by a highwayman who came home wounded one day and died there. Doors was replaced by New Farm.

The White House, originally of plasterwork with ornamental windows, was rebuilt by Edward Kennet in 1787, although he died before it was completed.

Friars farmhouse was rebuilt in 1796 in what later became Shoebury High Street, and North Shoebury Hall was entirely rebuilt in 1797 by John Gregory Welch.

The neighbouring manors of Great and Little Thorpe were purchased by Ynyr Burges between 1790-2, which gentleman and his heirs exerted much influence on the development of that neighbourhood for the next 200 years.

Five

Nineteenth-century Villages

Anticipating an invasion by Napoleon's forces from France, a manned signal station was set up on the shore at South Shoebury in 1798. This, along with those at Foulness and Great Wakering, was used to communicate with Sheerness and relayed messages to Lord Nelson's flagship anchored at the Nore, guarding the Thames. However, a report on the Thames defences acknowledged that the north shore was 'mainly mud' and therefore unattractive for beaching boats for the landing of troops.

Hundreds of volunteers had enlisted at the outbreak of the French wars and John Knapping of Suttons offered to raise a force in Great Wakering. His offer was refused as he could only find 50 men, while a minimum of 60 was needed for each company. However, a company was later formed with Joseph Knapping as captain and John Knapping as lieutenant.

In 1801, the population of North Shoebury was 202 persons; in South Shoebury the population was 101 (barely more than at the Domesday Survey, 700 years earlier). Parish registers from this time record only eight different occupations of men bringing their children to baptism: labourer, coastguard, looker, farmer, Lieutenant RN, waterman, fisherman and groom.

56 An early photograph of Shoeburyness High Street, looking south.

The villages themselves were little more than a few farms supplying the expanding neighbouring town of Southend and the markets of London. Poor harvests between 1776-1802 led to hard times for farmers and the labourers they employed and prompted both parishes to drain some of their marshes for wheat-growing land. This had the side-effect of improving people's health, as far as the ague was concerned. It has been said that Shoebury was the last place in Britain from which malaria disappeared.

Cockles became a popular catch for the local fishermen at this time, and prospects for fishermen were looking up. In 1854, John Baxter, a fish salesman of Billingsgate, leased all the fisheries on Southchurch and Shoebury shore from George Welch, the lord of those two manors, at an annual rent of £60. The neighbouring manors of Great and Little Thorpe, a contemporary wrote, 'abound with game and wildfowl'.

One particular fisherman was Joseph Cundy (1814-94), nicknamed Mr Punch. He was said once to have swum from Tilbury to Gravesend in chains for a bet. His home was an upturned ketch, originally a boat tackle store, on East Beach.

Both farm produce and fish continued to be transported to London by water rather than road. Regular hoy services ran from Shoebury to London transporting practically any goods, but mostly farm produce and bricks. For example, Howards of Great Wakering ran a hoy service until 1859 when it was taken over by J. Wright. The service ran from Wakering and Shoebury to Hartley's Wharf, Horsleydown on Monday, returning the following Wednesday.

Barge skippers could be commissioned to make purchases in London for local people, bringing them back on the return journey. Cargoes coming into Shoebury included coal, chalk and building materials for houses, roads and sea walls.

Samuel Benton, father of Philip, was responsible for rebuilding Moat Farm in 1824 and filling in part of the moat at the same time.

57   High Street, looking north, c.1915.

58 The 'new' promenade at East Beach. The barges pulled up on the beach behind may be unloading manure or chalk for the farmers' fields or waiting to collect bricks or hay.

In 1832, Mr Jones built the *Rampart Tavern* (later called the *Shoebury Tavern*) at the south end of the High Street. Initially this was little more than a large black wooden hut until it was altered into a large square room in 1847. On many an evening, Mr Stafford would entertain patrons with his violin. Another inn, called the *Men Found Out*, opened briefly nearby in 1849.

Coastguard

Poverty among the labourers continued to drive the smuggling trade and, in a bid to halt such illegal activities, the Customs Board established the Preventive Waterguard, a disciplined coastal force, in 1809. The force included the Riding Officers, who patrolled the coast to catch smugglers as they beached cargoes, and revenue cruisers who similarly watched for vessels illegally off-loading cargo.

In 1815, the Preventive Waterguard boat from Paglesham was relocated to Shoebury on the recommendation of the Customs Board's inspector. In 1816, the Preventive Waterguard was taken over by the Admiralty and withdrawn from the Kent coast in favour of shore-based naval crews. The Guard still operated on the Essex coast where, in about 1820, they were instructed to take responsibility at shipwrecks to safeguard cargoes and vessels from looters. The Admiralty, having considered both systems, favoured the Kent system of Coast Blockade as a reserve of trained seamen and recommended its use elsewhere.

59   Smith Street, *c.*1915.

60   Coastguard station, built in 1825 on the site of the Napoleonic signal station to protect ships and the shore from smugglers and wreckers, relocated to Shoebury Common in 1861. The shed in the foreground is a boathouse.

61   Coastguard station, seen here *c.*1900. Very few of the officers were local men.

In 1821, a Committee of Enquiry recommended that the Preventive Waterguard be controlled by the Board of Customs and, in January 1822, the Treasury accepted that proposal, noting that the new force would be called the Coast Guard (the name became coastguard in the 20th century), incorporating the waterguards, cutters and riding officers.

In 1825 a coastguard station and lookout with accommodation was built on Shoebury Common on the site of the Napoleonic signal station. It was an ideal location, having a wide view of the Thames and the numerous boats passing to the ports of Leigh, Tilbury or London. In addition, the station was close to the treacherous sandbanks and to the creeks and inlets around Paglesham and Foulness, which aided the smugglers in their crimes. Author A.E. Copping recorded that coastguard stations were 'ominously hung with guns, bayonets, pistols and other facilities for sudden human slaughter'. It was not a job for the faint-hearted.

In 1831, it was decided that the Board of Customs Coastguard should replace the Coast Blockade on the whole coast and the Admiralty won the right to appoint coastguard officers and to select boatmen from paid-off naval crews. The coastguard thus became a naval reserve and recruiting agency. Officers were unlikely to be recruited from the local population, to minimise the risk of collusion.

62   Shoebury Cottage, seen here *c*.1920, stood just east of the present Maplin Way and belonged to Major Burges. It was once the home of the Moorhouse family, owners of the Kursaal.

Within a decade, the coastguard was credited with greatly reducing smuggling, although their job by then was assisted by lower taxes.

In 1832, quarters to house 20 coastguards were built off Shoebury High Street in what later would become John Street.

In 1840, three miles of Shoebury's shore was strewn with timber and a gang of 100 men, said to be led by Mr Gardener, the Great Wakering postmaster, attempted to carry it away. The coastguards had to fire warning shots to disperse the gang. However, in 1844, most of the coastguards were transferred to Leigh where the need for a deterrent against smuggling was greater. Five years later the Admiralty sold the redundant buildings at Shoebury to the Ordnance Board, although they remained as tenants in the western half of the building for a few more years. All but a tiny portion of the 1825 coastguard cottages was demolished in 1898.

The coastguard service returned to Shoebury in 1861 when a new station was erected behind Shoebury common (now the site of Thorpe Bay yacht club).

Poor Laws

In 1801, the household furniture at the North Shoebury workhouse was valued at £106 10s., including plate. A notable temporary resident there was Sarah Davy, born to William the baker of Great Wakering about 1800. She worked at *The Anchor*, Great Wakering and then the *Red Lion*, from where she progressed to being a scullery maid at North Shoebury Hall. While there, she contracted typhus and was sent to the North Shoebury workhouse. On her recovery she obtained domestic positions in Southend, Rochford and then in London. There she met and married Washington Shirley, 8th Earl of Ferrers, and about 30 years her senior, making Sarah the Countess of Ferrers and a very wealthy woman.

At the North Shoebury parish vestry meeting held on 4 June 1832 Peter Burchell, the churchwarden, and Henry Mason, the overseer, were charged with finding some alternative accommodation for 'the poor now residing in the tenements in the workhouse yard in consequence of a notice received to quit'. The officers were further asked to dispose of all the workhouse furniture, goods and chattels by public auction. The records give no further details about the fate of the evicted paupers.

1834 saw the establishment of Poor Law Unions, which became responsible for the poor and sick of a group of parishes, and both North and South Shoebury became part of the Rochford Union.

Local men James Banyard, William Chipperfield and James Glasscock became Guardians of the Poor, responsible for the vulnerable members of their parishes. By 1838 the Well House (also known as Well Marsh Cottage) in Ness Road, a small cottage adjacent to the

public well, had been donated to 'the poor of Shoebury'. It had been built by John Knapping of Suttons for his steward in 1829. Cattle would be brought to drink at the nearby pond and paid a ha'penny per head per week. John Knapping died in 1833, aged 68.

The redundant Shoebury workhouse, High House, narrowly avoided being blown down in a terrific gale in 1836, which levelled immense numbers of trees and buildings. High House was put up for sale on 1 March 1849, at which time it was a freehold property divided into three tenements with a brewhouse and wash-house. It was purchased by Christopher Parsons for £320.

High House appears to have been somewhat unlucky and it was destroyed by fire on 14/15 September 1877. The *Southend Standard* reported: 'The Royal Artillery fire brigade attended but the building and furniture were all ablaze already. The fire was extinguished but nearly everything was destroyed.'

63   High Street. The Methodist Church can be seen on the right-hand side of the street.

The black weather-boarded Pyghtle cottage next door was sold to Miss Knapping in 1885 for £410 and was subsequently used as a farm cottage, then as a private house, owned by the May family for some 100 years.

St Andrew's

William Henry King, then tenant of Suttons, Chapmans and Cherrytree Farm and John Knapping's stepson, expressed concern about St Andrew's church in 1847 as 15th-century glass brought from the continent by the late rector, the Rev. Masey, had been replaced with cheap local glass. King wrote: 'It is evident that within a few years, many more of the subjects will be destroyed or much damaged unless proper means are taken to preserve them. This I pointed out to the churchwarden personally who, although acquiescing in the truth of my

remarks will never, I believe, attend to my suggestions.'

The original small Norman windows had been replaced with stained glass but, as King had predicted, this was taken out during the 1852 restoration – the then rector, the Rev. Philip Wynne Yorke, gave it to his manservant. A memorial window of painted glass was inserted in its place.

The Rev. Yorke, rector of St Andrew's from 1811, was the last resident of the rectory at The Grove, north of the present Campfield Road. He enjoyed the company of the garrison officers and would treat them to drives in his coach and four greys, which were admired throughout the countryside. Benton likened him to a 'kindly squire and parson in one' as, with no resident squire, Yorke fulfilled some of the duties of that position. He was known for

64 Interior of the first St Peter's Church, South Shoebury, a corrugated iron hall erected in Dane Street in 1899. In 1911, this building was moved on rollers to Hinguar Street where it served as the church hall for the new St Peter's.

65 View from Ness Road to St Andrew's, South Shoebury Hall and the Sunshine Home.

dispensing both spiritual and medicinal support and died in 1858.

Brick Making

By the mid-19th century, the eastern parts of the Rochford Hundred were described as being 'low lying but exceedingly fertile'. However, despite the soil's fertility, poor harvests and falling wheat prices were encouraging farmers to seek alternative ways to make money from their land. John Daines, a tenant farmer at Bournes Green, wrote in about 1850 that 'agricultural prospects are dreadful in our neighbourhood'.

There was a great demand for bricks in the 19th century, both in rapidly expanding Southend and London, and Shoebury combined all the elements necessary for a successful brickmaking business: a deep layer of brickearth (wind-blown clay), sand, water, fuel and easy access to London.

By the late 1840s, John Knapping's grandson, Dale (named with his grandmother's maiden name), set up the Shoeburyness Brick Company and established a small brickfield with four stalls and a washmill behind Suttons house, of which he was the tenant. Three experienced moulders, Messrs Stafford, Avery and Knott, were brought over from Kent to make high quality red bricks, although yellow stock bricks became characteristic of the buildings in Shoebury, sometimes with red brick detailing. Edward Cook became the manager of the site.

Brickearth was dug by hand in the winter months and transferred to an 8ft-deep circular washmill. Here the clay was vigorously agitated in water and mixed with pulverised chalk, creating a substance called malm. The larger particles sank, allowing the liquid malm to be pumped into 8ft-high brick 'boxes' (washbacks) by pipeline, where it would be left to dry. A temperer would separate organic matter from cinders by sieving incinerated household rubbish and lay it two feet deep over the malm. The clay and ash would then be fed into a hopper or pugmill and mixed, ready for a skilled moulder to form the bricks. The barrow loader would take the bricks to be

66   East Beach, showing the barge-landing piers used by the brickworks. Benton describes the 19th-century out-
look from Shoebury as presenting 'an endless variety of craft … Everyday the largest and most splendid ships may
be seen passing.'

laid on off-bearing barrows to be sun dried. Finally, an open-air kiln (clamp) based on a matrix of old bricks would be built up to a 15ft-high pyramid by four crowders throwing the 'green' bricks up to the man above. A fire was lit underneath and it was left to burn for up to 20 days. This method produced yellow London Stock bricks.

The acrid fumes of smouldering brick kilns became a familiar smell across the town. Searle wrote: 'The most nauseating fumes often arise from the stocks of bricks made and burned in this manner, which tends to make the immediate neighbourhood of one of these clamps anything but a desirable place for a residence.' Similarly, Benton said: 'The brickfields … are not an attractive feature and much of the neighbourhood has lost its rural character.'

In the early days, scrub and broom from the common was used as fuel but, as the brickfields expanded, coal was brought by barge from London. Initially, horses were used to turn the washmills and transport the finished bricks.

The brickfields soon extended along what is now East Beach, incorporating several fields formerly belonging to South Shoebury Hall and Friars Farm, becoming known as the Shorefield works. A second site, the Model works, developed either side of Elm Road from c.1859, the washmills to the south, stables and workers' cottages (Earthpit Cottages) north of the road. A series of wells were bored for convenient water supply.

The Shoebury brickworks developed rapidly throughout the 1850 and '60s and represent one of the major and longest used brick-making areas in the Rochford Hundred. By 1861, the workers were employed from 4am to 8pm, producing 50,000 bricks each week, those from the Shorefield works marked DKP (Dale Knapping Proprietors).

At its height, the Shorefield brickworks had 16 berths and 32 washbacks (also called settling ponds or malm banks). The Model field was smaller, having eight berths and 12 washbacks. Together, the Shoebury brickfields employed up to 1,000 people and produced 28 million bricks annually, most of which were sold in London.

When the military established themselves in Shoeburyness local demand rocketed. Brickworkers would transport bricks by wheelbarrow directly to the garrison building site for one shilling a day.

By the 1870s engines were used in some of the washmills, and chain drivers began to replace horses. The finished bricks were taken

67 Brickfield stables, just north of Elm Road. Horses were crucial to the early brickworks, turning the washmills and transporting bricks to the barges waiting at the loading piers on East Beach.

by narrow gauge railway lines, owned by the brick companies, to the beach where they were loaded onto barges for transportation. At one point, Knapping's company owned the biggest fleet of sailing barges on the Thames.

68 Barge piers at East Beach, c.1920. Notice the stack of bricks, back left, waiting to be loaded onto barges.

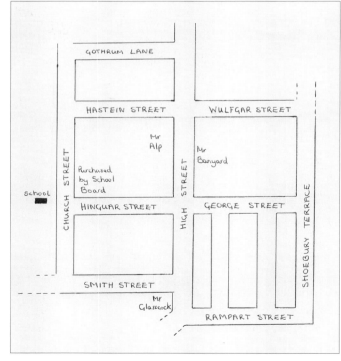

69 East Beach and Sawkins blacksmiths. The blacksmith's on East Beach was kept busy shoeing the brickfield horses, as well as making equipment for barge owners.

70 Plan of the proposed development of Shoebury village, by John Hopkins, 1857. The laying of the railway in 1884 altered the map completely. Many of the first plots developed (John Street and Dane Street) were owned by George Smith.

The brickfields owe a great deal of their growth and prosperity to the availability of cheap water transport and the proximity, via the river, of the London market. The small, roughly-built spritsail barges were ideal for the job, their shallow draughts enabling loading close to the shore from low piers. Barges carried between 30-35,000 bricks per trip, representing one day's work for a four-man loading gang, although in later years the barges were gradually replaced by railways.

His fortune made, Knapping sold his works to J. Jackson & Co, who sold it on to Eastwoods Ltd. In 1889, a six-week strike was called when 15 diggers were refused a pay rise at Eastwood's brickfields, resulting in a lock-out of 60-70 men and hungry times for their families.

Both the brickworks sites were still being worked in 1896, although the Shorefield/East Beach site closed soon after the First World War. In 1932 the Milton Hall Brick Company acquired land at Star Lane and extended their brickearth extractions across Poynters Lane to North Shoebury. The Elm Road brickworks operated into the 1950s and brickearth extraction north of Elm Road continued throughout the 1970s.

'Steps' between road and field boundaries today from Elm Road to Poynters Lane mark the edge of the clay extraction area. For many years, brick rubble was a common find on the beach and the stumps of old piles, the last vestiges of the barge piers, remained a hazard to small boats. The Shorefield site is now a car park behind East Beach; the Model field is mostly under housing and the Vanguards Industrial Estate.

At first, the brickfields had a slow impact on the local population and the 1851 census shows that 40 of the 158 inhabitants of South Shoebury had been born locally. In North Shoebury, 61 of the 192 residents had been born there. The population of Great Wakering was 880 and that of Southchurch 455.

As workers were attracted by employment on the brickfields, developers began to see the potential of South Shoebury. George Smith, William Alp and John Hopkins were among the first to purchase land for residential development.

More importantly, at the same time as the rise of the brickfields, Shoebury caught the eye of the War Department as a potential weapons testing site – the history of the little village was soon to change irrevocably.

Six
Military Invasion

In *Shoeburyness and the Guns*, Barry wrote, '… Shoeburyness is a dreary place … the broadest and most sterile foreshore perhaps in England.' However, it is that very characteristic that led to Shoebury becoming one of the most important places in the country.

In 1805 England's primary practice artillery range was on the Plumstead Marshes at Woolwich but, that year, Lt-Colonel Henry Shrapnel, inventor of the shrapnel shell, journeyed from Woolwich to try out his new explosive shell at Shoebury. Following Shrapnel's successful visit, the attention of the authorities was drawn to the possibilities of the area as a permanent practice site, as the firing at Woolwich was interfering with the increasingly busy shipping lanes of the Thames. Shoebury's wide, flat landscape was just what they were looking for.

The Director General of Artillery visited Shoebury in May 1845 to investigate the expanse of sand where firing could take place at both high and low tide and enable missiles to be found and recovered after firing. He reported back that six vacant coastguard cottages and several unoccupied buildings at Rampart House Farm were available and would be suitable for accommodation.

The first tracts of land were purchased by the War Department in April 1849, initially extending to some 45 acres, consisting of a strip of grassy coast bordering a lonely stretch of seashore. There was some delay in purchasing land owned by the trustees of the late Mr Pattison as one of them had hesitated to sign the deed "upon conscientious scruples as he is adverse to all measures connected with War

and Warlike operations …". The Rev. James Montagu, the curate at Sutton Hall, wrote: 'The ground purchased is mostly wild, rough common honeycombed with rabbit holes. I have seen snipe and woodcock shot there.'

In July 1849, a small party of nine men together with a sergeant of the Sappers and Miners and their officer, Lieutenant A. Fisher of the Engineers, arrived to select a site for use as a temporary Experimental Establishment. The men themselves were accommodated in a campsite, while Lt Fisher used one of the vacant coastguard cottages.

The first gunners to arrive at Shoebury were an advance party of 8 Company, 4 Battalion Garrison Artillery from Woolwich under Corporal Hanna, followed by half the remainder of the company commanded by Captain George Hyde. The first military activity saw the RSM and probably the Royal Artillery preparing a practice battery for small bored muzzle loading guns in early autumn 1849.

That first year, however, the men returned to Woolwich for the winter months, leaving just a small maintenance party behind. St Andrew's registers record that the first garrison baby, James, born to James Burns, Gunner and Driver R.A., and his wife Isabella, was baptised on 21 December 1849.

This set the pattern for the next five years, with testing conducted at Shoebury only during the summer.

As numbers of soldiers visiting Shoebury increased, so did the village of tents, with officers finding billets in local cottages, or in Southend hotels, four miles away. Fisher was both sociable

71 Village children pose for a photograph at the garrison main entrance, *c.*1905.

72 Coupe's stores at the garrison main entrance. The Royal Artillery presented a clock to William Coupe on his retirement in 1891 for his 'never failing kindness, urbanity, energy and punctuality' in his position as postmaster.

73 The camp field. The first soldiers to arrive at Shoebury were accommodated in tents, hence the name of Campfield Road. The same bell tents were used for the competitors who arrived each year for the National Artillery Competition.

and athletic, described by the Rev. Wynne Yorke as 'a delightful fellow, a wonderfully speedy runner'. He lost no time in setting up tennis courts and introduced himself to the society of Dale Knapping, Captain Baldwin the coastguard officer, and the Rev. Yorke. Fisher eventually married Carrie Eden, the daughter of the rector of Leigh. The Rev. Montagu welcomed the influx of new blood to the sleepy village; he became a familiar face around the garrison site, conducting church services in the barracks before the soldiers built their own church. He would also collect shopping for the families, delivering it in his trap when he visited the garrison on Sundays, taking great interest in life there and noting details in his diaries. For example: 'The rabbits enticed the cats and there was a certain gunner, a noted shikari against the

tabbies who had a hearth rug of their skins.'

The first recorded trial at Shoebury involved the stickless rockets invented by William Hale. Christopher Parsons wrote in his diary on 21 January 1847: '… to Shoebury Ness to see some Rocket firing, the invention of Mr Hailes.' The trial was repeated in 1850 for a contingent of officers from Woolwich, with a rangeline pegged out at 4,000 yards and a spectacular demonstration of the metal projectile powered by seven 10-pound rocket motors. Local boys found one of the two missiles three or four miles away.

Later that year, proposals for construction of a permanent wood stove and a coal yard were rejected by the Board of Ordnance. Similarly, they refused to finance the building of accommodation for women and children, suggesting that, if the women could not be housed in the existing buildings, the Barrack Master could requisition another tent. Shoebury was still considered as only a temporary site.

There was early disagreement between the military and locals over the ownership of Maplin Sands. Local fishermen, in particular, objected to the military use of the land as it interfered with their fishing, which had been carried on for generations. The situation did not improve over the next 30 years and culminated in costly litigation.

Experiments during 1851 were described as being held 'on an extended scale [and had]

determined the merits of various guns and of several kinds of concussion shells submitted by various investors … Practice commences at about half ebb and can be continued until an hour after flood; that is four or five hours each tide.' A look-out party was stationed three miles from the battery to watch for the fall of the missile and record the time, deflection of the shot, and its rebound. They communicated by semaphore. Large weapons were brought to Shoebury by barge and landed on the beach, but it wasn't until 1856/7 that a convenient landing pier was constructed.

The first major development of the site was a proper mess facility on the eastern end of the

74 The Old Battery, *c.*1880. The track running right later became Mess Road.

75 Soldiers at work in 1887 at the 'Repository Berth', where cranes were installed to lift heavy guns and equipment on and off barges.

coastguard station in 1852, including a kitchen and servants quarters. This was followed by a proper barracks building, black weather-boarded huts just inside the garrison gate, to replace the camp of tents. Part of the old Rampart farmhouse was used as a hospital.

The arrival of the soldiers attracted tradesmen to South Shoebury and in 1852 Messrs Chesterman took over the *Shoebury Tavern* adjacent to the army lands. The Director General of Artillery was concerned that further

development in this area would be detrimental to the discipline of his troops and '… extremely inconvenient on every account'. Consequently, two additional plots of land were purchased in February 1853 to prevent their being developed for housing.

1853 saw eight companies spending four to six weeks at Shoebury. The sound of gunfire began to be regularly heard as the smooth bore 32lb muzzle-loading weapons were tested. Vessels passing in the estuary were warned by signal flags to keep clear of the firing zone while tests were conducted over the sandy flats. However, in 1854, a bathing party from Southend was lucky to escape injury while watching a firing practice when a gun exploded, killing three sergeants. The following year, two 16-year-old boys from Great Wakering were killed by a live shell they found on the beach. The Rev. Montagu's dog, Ginger, had a lucky escape when he was hit in the leg by shrapnel.

The outbreak of the Crimean War in 1854 increased the urgency for weaponry testing and Shoebury began to see activity all year round, with a series of landing piers built 1856/7 to facilitate the arrival of men and equipment. 'Royal Artillery' as a job description of fathers began to dominate the South Shoebury parish baptismal registers.

At this time, the road to Great Wakering passed via Suttons, Cherrytree Farm, Barnfleet and Cupids Corner. The route to Southend ran along Elm Road, the main public road, and then through North Shoebury. The military establishment was connected to Elm Road via a private track with a public right of way, running past Friars Farm. This track (later to become the High Street) was gated in three places along its length, regularly in a bad state of repair and continued to cause complaints from locals and the military alike. The track was often impassable after rain, its condition exacerbated by the 'heavy traffic' from Mr Alp's farm (Friars) and Mr Knapping's brickworks.

The problems came to a head in the winter of 1855-6 when local tradesmen refused to deliver to the army land and soldiers could not walk to St Andrew's church. Therefore, the military

76 Royal Horse Artillery horse, near wheeler of team, near side, pictured at Shoebury garrison in 1863. In the early years, horses were the only means of transporting heavy equipment around the ranges and became a familiar sight exercising in the village.

77   West gate entrance to barracks on Central Road, with sentry box.

78   Central Road, originally a public right of way, later called Chapel Road. Notice the clock tower covered with ivy.

79   An early picture of Campfield Road, built in the 1880s. This view looks west towards Ness Road, with the railway crossing gates in the foreground.

approved a separate road to the barracks. In 1856 the Ordnance Board constructed a new road from the Barrack gate to the beach, later named Rampart Street. Secondly, in 1857, following lengthy discussions with landowners, a new road, Central Road (later called Chapel Road), was constructed north-west from the barracks to Ness Road. This new road remained a right of way for pedestrians and farm wagons until the 1880s, when the Government built Campfield Road as an alternative route. Ownership of Campfield Road passed to the local authority in 1920.

Although experiments rapidly became a regular feature of Shoebury, it was not until 1855 that the facility was considered permanent and the post of Superintendent of Experiments formally instituted. The first to hold that post was Lt-Col. Mitchell who was unhappy that he was unable to find lodgings any nearer than Southend.

In 1856, a clock tower, gatehouse, guardroom, cells and offices were built. It was said that the

clock tower was needed because the firing of the guns damaged everyone's pocket watches and no one ever knew the time. Mounted artillerymen exercising their horses became a familiar feature in the village.

Further building works on the site in 1856-7 included Beach House for the second officer, quarters for three staff sergeants and a hospital. The hospital contained four general wards, a surgery with separate facilities for fever, casualty, an isolation ward and mortuary. It is thought that Florence Nightingale herself came to inspect the new hospital. Its builders, George Smith & Sons, were responsible for George Street, John Street and Smith Street in the village.

On 1 April 1859, following a proposal by a committee of Royal Artillery officers that '... a more eligible place could scarcely be found', the School of Gunnery was officially established for 'individual improvement as well as for the advancement of Artillery Science'. The staff comprised a commandant, field officer, chief instructor, three gunnery instructors, a

80 The clocktower and guardoom (left) were built between 1860-2. The clock was necessary as gunfire noise kept damaging everyone's pocket watches.

81 Officers CDG Batteries RHA, September 1863. Six officers' quarters overlooking the cricket field were nick-named 'bloke row', bloke being a naval term for a senior rank.

brigade major and 16 other officers, storekeepers and support staff.

At about this time, the adoption of rifles and armoured warships necessitated investigations into the theory and practice of a new form of warfare. The battle between gun and armour was, according to Major Tony Hill, 'largely fought on the marshes at Shoeburyness'. Powered cranes were installed to manoeuvre the massive new guns. The village certainly knew when these guns were being tested; one 81-ton gun, for example, shattered all the windows in the village and caused doors to burst from their hinges.

The Duke of Cambridge, a cousin of Queen Victoria and Commander in Chief of the army (1856–95), made frequent visits to Shoeburyness to observe the trials.

82 H Battery RHA, September 1863. More than 60 military graves are in St Andrew's churchyard.

83   The garrison church of St Peter and St Paul was built in 1866 as a chapel school, but was never used as a school. It is built of ragstone with a slate roof.

84   Horseshoe Barracks, built 1860.

85 The Commandant's house was built in 1855 by D. Nicholson & Sons of Wandsworth for the Superintendent. It became the Commandant's House in 1859 on the formation of the School of Gunnery. The conservatory was lost in the 1987 hurricane.

In 1860 the military purchased more land from the Bristow estate, increasing their land holdings to 200 acres. Successful purchases included a six-acre plot containing the rectory at The Grove and a new rectory was built at the government's expense south-west of St Andrew's (near the present Ulster Avenue).

By this time there were 180 troops living in the garrison barrack block, while Shoebury village itself had been swelled by literally hundreds of building contractors. Existing wells were supplemented by a new freshwater supply laid on to the garrison, which also benefited the village. A borehouse was provided, together with a brick-supported storage tower holding 50,000 gallons. A pumping station was built in Elm Road in the mid-1890s.

New brick artillery barracks, designed by Capt. T. Inglis RE, were laid out in 1860 in a unique

86 The staff of the Officers' Mess *c.*1890, including Myra Rivers (centre).

87 Band practice at the garrison, 1907. The band of the 1st Essex Royal Garrison Artillery (Volunteers) was considered the finest in Essex and, with the gunners, provided guards of honour for many prestigious occasions. The band regularly headed the annual mayoral church parade at Southend.

semi-circle around a parade ground, known as Horseshoe Barracks. Each of the six barrack blocks accommodated 96 men in eight rooms, with two rooms at each end for sergeants.

At the 1861 census there were 191 unmarried members of the Royal Artillery resident at Shoeburyness Garrison with an average age of 24 years. They included two 14-year-old trumpeters, John Marshall and James McCormick.

The War Office gave an allowance for a priest in 1862 and Fr John Moore came to minister to Catholics in both Southend and Shoeburyness. This entailed walking from Southend and back, although, later, the army supplied a horse and cab to take him home. Shoebury's first Catholic church, St George's, was little more than a hut built in Ness Road in 1862; it was rebuilt in 1891 and again in 1939.

Anglican services were held in the drill shed until the garrison's own church was built in 1866 and dedicated to St Peter and St Paul in 1891. The military established their own school to cater for the soldiers' children.

From 1865, Shoeburyness was selected by the National Artillery Association as a competition range. Every August, hundreds of competitors from all over Britain moved into a village of tents on and around the garrison site to compete for prizes, the most prestigious of which was the Queen's prize of £100. By the 1880s, over 1,000 men were accommodated under canvas each year on Waterworks Meadow opposite St Andrew's church and Campfield between Hinguar Street and the garrison.

At the garrison a cricket field, attractively surrounded by chestnut and sycamore trees, joined Lt Fisher's tennis courts. Volunteer soldiers and locals joined together to perform sketches and concerts and a stage was erected in the drill shed. The first play was performed in 1866, with the Rev. Yorke and Alfred Wedd lending their horses and traps to ferry people to the event. Thus began a tradition and a permanent theatre building was erected in 1884.

The annual report by Henry Smith M.D., Surgeon Major, commented in 1867 that the rooms at Shoeburyness were kept clean and that the men bathed regularly in the sea. The routine was for four hours of drill in the winter with an additional hour in the summer. Recreation facilities included a gym, ball courts, skittle and bowling alleys, cricket and football pitches, a recreation room and library with lectures and concerts laid on in the winter months. The canteen was '… admirably managed and the supplies have been of the best quality.' The average number of permanent residents at garrison was two hundred. Smith also noted that at the time cholera was prevalent in southern England, sanitary conditions at the garrison and the village prevented a local outbreak. However, W.F. Noble attributed the parish's escape from cholera to the natural good drainage of the area.

In 1869 brick married quarters were erected to house increasing numbers of soldiers and two small upper rooms at the eastern end of the old coastguard terrace became the first officers' mess. The original 'black hut' barracks also became married quarters. Officers' quarters were built in Warrior Square Road.

88 This 1907 pillow fight between men mounted on a comrade's shoulders appears to have been enjoyed by all ranks.

The Well House in Ness Road, formerly owned by the Guardians of the Poor of Rochford, was acquired by the military in 1870, the couple who had been living there for some 25 years being paid £5 to vacate the property. The building was refurbished as a married soldiers' quarters but in 1878 Major Lambert had the building pulled down and rebuilt with a red tiled roof. This cottage, too, was pulled down in 1930 when the road was widened.

The size of the guns being tested was constantly increasing to compete with developments in iron-clad warships and armour plating. The garrison's own jetty was built in 1870 to receive explosives and ammunition for the Proof and Experimental Establishment, direct from the Woolwich arsenal.

The final extension of the garrison site took in land north of Campfield Road on which a two-storey terrace of married quarters was built.

The band of the 1st Essex Royal Garrison Artillery (Volunteers) was considered the finest in Essex and, with the gunners, provided guards of honour for many prestigious occasions, such as the opening of East Ham town hall by King George V. They took part in Queen Victoria's volunteer review in Horse Guards Parade in 1898 with regiments from all over the UK.

Locally, the band regularly headed the annual mayoral church parade at Southend.

Since their arrival at the site, military correspondence cited the location of the establishment as 'Shoebury Ness', which gradually evolved into 'Shoeburyness' and became adopted by the locals. This, more than anything, indicates the vast influence the garrison had on the development of the little parish of South Shoebury.

Ten years after the military had first arrived at Shoeburyness, South Shoebury's population was growing as fast as that of Southend, and by 1861 stood at 1,080 (plus 394 in the garrison). Altogether there were 957 males and 517 females in the parish. W.F. Noble wrote that South Shoebury was 'once dull, quiet and marshy, overrun with furze and rabbits ... but now ever lively'.

North Shoebury, he probably would have said, was still 'dull and quiet', continuing much as it had done for centuries as a predominantly agricultural parish, its chief crops being wheat, barley, peas and beans. In fact, in all but name, North Shoebury was much more closely allied with Great Wakering than South Shoebury.

The garrison had certainly put Shoeburyness on the map. However, there were members of the community of whom Shoebury can be as proud as of any of its military achievements.

Seven

Gentlemen of the Community

Apart from the soldiers and their families, builders and craftsmen arrived to construct the garrison, while shopkeepers and tradesmen moved in to serve the expanding population.

The growth of South Shoebury benefited people like agricultural labourer James Lincoln and his wife who were able to provide lodgings for a bricklayer and four painters. In fact, most of the labourers, out of necessity, became lodgers with the local population. Those with similar trades tended to stick together, and the 1861 census shows, for example, homes with five carpenters lodging there and, next door, five brickmakers. The families hailed from all over Britain.

Amongst all the resident labourers, there was only one professional plumber in the whole of North and South Shoebury — an indication of the extent of the piped water supply.

In 1861 many families were large, regardless of the size of their homes. For example, agricultural labourer Joseph Keys had five sons and two daughters. To help support the family, his wife Martha took in washing and a lodger shared their small cottage. Also in South Shoebury, brickmaker Thomas Osborne had five daughters and four sons; the household included his wife and three lodgers. Similarly, brickmaker William Barrett had a wife, seven sons, one daughter and three lodgers in his cottage in the High Street.

Among the newcomers were two police constables: 20-year-old James Brooks and 24-year-old married man, Jesse Edwards, who replaced PC Smith, no.203.

Life as a soldier may have been dangerous but offered compensations that other Shoebury

employments did not. For example, George Forum, originally from Ireland, was 52 years old; he was living on a Royal Artillery pension with his 27-year-old wife. Daniel Bowman, meanwhile, lived with his bargeman son and family while working full-time as an agricultural labourer — he was 82 years old.

South Shoebury High Street in 1860 included grocers, butchers, bakers, drapers, chandlers and, of course, the *Shoebury Tavern*, then run by James Kirkwood and his wife, Martha. Kirkwood employed a housekeeper and a barman while his 16-year-old daughter, also called Martha, worked as a waitress at the inn.

Thomas Laslett, born in Kent, was in charge of the grocer's shop at Parson's Corner and was also a coal merchant. There was a letterbox in the wall, from where post was collected at 4.30pm. The village blacksmith's was run by three men, all named William Wolfe: father, son and nephew. Much of the blacksmiths' work would have been the shoeing of horses and making the metalwork for their harnesses. However, there were also farm implements to make, locks and hinges and iron rims for wagon wheels, as well as pots and pans for domestic use. A good blacksmith doubled as a farrier, caring for horses' feet. The blacksmith was key to the village economy where so many livelihoods depended on agriculture and agriculture depended on horses. This grocer's and blacksmiths' was the sum total of tradesmen at North Shoebury.

Edward Wynne became rector of St Andrew's in 1858 and moved into the new rectory south-west of the church. He had been born in Kent and had married Annie, 22 years his junior. Two

89   High Street, South Shoebury. In 1841, 90 per cent of the population were born locally; in 1871 this had fallen to 10 per cent.

90   Rampart Street (pictured here c.1920), John Street and Dane Street were the first residential streets of South Shoebury. In 1861, the coastguards were quartered in Rampart Street.

91   Soldiers' Home, 37 High Street. This photograph was taken in 1897.

92   Henry Kirby's stores, West Road, opened in 1898.

93 The vicarage, North Shoebury.

nursemaids cared for their two sons, while the family also employed a housemaid and a groom. In 1862, the Wynnes were blessed with the birth of a daughter, Evelyn, who later married Captain Goold-Adams.

At North Shoebury vicarage Joseph Commyns, born in Penzance, lived with wife Deborah and their daughter, Emma. They employed a housemaid, plus Mr and Mrs Pettit, their groom and cook.

William Coupe was South Shoebury's postmaster during the 1870s–'80s, also advertising himself as a chemist and stationer. He received letters from Southend at 6.35am and 12 noon and despatched outgoing letters at 9.00am and 4.25pm. The Royal Artillery presented Coupe a clock on his retirement in 1891 for his 'never failing kindness, urbanity, energy and punctuality'.

Christopher Parsons

The Parsons family were important landowners in south-east Essex for many generations. An early Christopher Parsons who farmed Great and Little Thorpe and owned the Shore House died on 22 March 1713 and is buried at Southchurch.

94 Coupe's stores, South Shoebury. The roof of the garrison theatre can just be seen, far right.

The grandson of the above was the Christopher Parsons who built the famous Parsons Barn at North Shoebury Hall (see Chapter 4). Soon afterwards, Parsons became the tenant of North Shoebury House, then owned by John Ibbetson. While Ibbetson built a brick front onto the house (leading to its alternative name Bricked House), Parsons was responsible for extending the house at the back. He died in 1787 aged 88 and is buried in North Shoebury chancel with his wife Catherine (née Kennet). Ibbetson died in 1804 and also rests in St Mary's chancel, beneath the epitaph: 'Just, generous, good, a virtuous life he passed. Beloved, esteemed, respected to the last'.

The next Christopher Parsons married three times. Firstly in 1759 to Susannah Whale of Little Wakering who died in 1769 aged thirty.

95   Christopher Parsons, 1807-82.

Secondly, to widow Elizabeth Woodward of South Shoebury, who died in 1778 aged thirty-nine. His third wife was Elizabeth Joscelyne, whom he married in 1779. This Parsons spent some time as tenant of South Shoebury Hall. He died in 1804 and Elizabeth in 1841.

On Parsons' death, the Shoebury property was bequeathed to his son, yet again Christopher Parsons who was then living at the Lawn, Southchurch (now Alleyn Court School). This Parsons married Lucy Asplin of Little Wakering Hall and died in 1869.

His son, the fifth Christopher Parsons, was born in 1807 at The Lawn. Like his forebears, Parsons became a tenant farmer, moving to North Shoebury Hall after the death of his widowed grandmother who had been living there. He remained there from 1842-82, employing 14 men and three boys to work the farm.

Farmer by trade, Parsons' hobby was natural history. He was a member of the Linnaean Society and is credited with discovering the first native specimen of the Essex Emerald moth. Parsons spent hours walking the local area, between 1825-79 collecting 319 native plant species. His collections, all carefully dated and labelled, include several species that are now rare in Britain. For example, Pheasant's Eye (*Adonis anua*) is not found in Essex at all now. The coastal flora of the Shoebury area is of enormous botanical importance and Parsons' collection indicates how much has been lost in little over 100 years, such as the Sea Bindweed (*Calystegia solanella*) he found on Shoebury Common in 1826. His notes include daily meteorological observations, while his diaries provide a detailed account of a Victorian gentleman's lifestyle, and his collections are now prized exhibits of Southend Museum.

Parsons married Anne Jane Silversides in 1840 but she suffered poor health and died of typhus in 1847. However, Parsons' diaries demonstrate the active social life he continued

96   North Shoebury Hall, *c.*1910. Christopher Parsons lived here from 1842-82.

to lead – mainly in the company of bachelors of North Shoebury, Arthur Wedd of Barnhouses and Samuel Benton. They enjoyed trips to London theatres, catching a steam ship from one of the loading piers at Southend or travelling by carriage to Brentwood to catch the train.

Shooting parties were popular, often to Foulness where Parsons owned land. For example, in September 1850, with his cousin Charles Asplin, he bagged 12 brace of birds, four rabbits and a hare. Guns came in handy, too, for controlling the local rook population. Parsons also rode with the Essex Union hounds.

Shoebury's flat landscape was ideal for hare coursing, with young men following the hunt for miles on foot and more genteel participants in carts. The hunts were often organised by Edward Jackson of Rayleigh and his team of foot beagles which, Benton recorded, did much for the 'enjoyment and health of the whole district'. In October 1874, the Prince Imperial, grandson of Napoleon, then training at the garrison, joined the hunt along with officers, cadets and some undergraduates from Oxford and Cambridge.

Less energetically, Parsons spent at least one day a year at home brewing or bottling wine. He also served on the Board of Guardians of the Rochford Poor Law Union.

Parsons married his second wife, Mary Benton, on 5 December 1850 at St Mary's, following which his social life was transformed. Notably, his dinners with Mary's bachelor brother, Samuel, were replaced with dinners with her married older brother, Philip (the historian), and other married couples. Outings included visiting Shoeburyness to watch the firing trials.

Excavations at North Shoebury Hall show that the couple kept ornamental gardens on the south side of the house, including two steep-sided, flat-based pits lined with tiles. These were typical of beds prepared for fruit trees, the tiles restricting root growth and, therefore, the eventual size of the trees.

97   Parsons Corner, c.1950. In 1940 Arthur Mee said of North Shoebury: 'A few scattered farms and cottages survive on the broad flat acres here.'

Parsons moved back to The Lawn in February 1882, where he died that September aged 75. He left no heirs and his property was divided among six cousins. The shop and cottages at Parsons Corner were sold to Mrs E. Knapping of South Shoebury Hall. Parsons is buried with other members of his family in St Mary's churchyard.

Philip Benton

Philip Benton was born 1 November 1815 at North Shoebury House, Poynters Lane and was baptised four days later, the third of six children born to Samuel and Charlotte Benton.

On 10 October 1843, Benton married Eliza Squier (b.1818), daughter of tenant farmer Joseph Squier of East Horndon. The couple moved to Beauchamps, Shopland, which they rented from Benton's father, inheriting it on his death in 1847. Benton also farmed Burton's Farm in Barling, again owned by his father, and later Little Wakering Hall. They had nine children: Charlotte, Philip, Samuel, William, Mary Louisa, Elizabeth, Frances, Charles and Edward. Eldest daughter, Charlotte, married a cousin of Christopher Parsons.

Benton actively participated in parish affairs at Shopland, serving as overseer of the poor from 1845-51 and in 1881. He was also surveyor of the highways from 1852-82 and churchwarden from 1868-85. When Benton's daughters married, he not only provided a reception for the wedding guests, followed by a 'carpet dance' at home that evening, but also organised a supper for all his workmen and labourers and gave gifts to all his tenants and poorer friends.

Like his friend and brother-in-law Christopher Parsons, Philip Benton had a deep interest in local history and by 1860 was giving lectures on English history at Southend and Rochford.

In 1866 Benton and family moved to Little Wakering Hall, as a tenant of John Tyrell, where they lived until 1885. Soon after this move, Philip set about detailing a complete history of the Rochford Hundred, working from 1867–88 by tackling each parish separately in alphabetical order. He had barely completed *North Shoebury* when crippling arthritis of his hands at the age of 73 forced him to abandon the task.

The completed parishes, originally published as 58 pamphlets, have since been amalgamated into two volumes, *The History of the Rochford Hundred*. A contemporary (1874) reviewer declared, 'It is a book that should be in the possession of every householder in the county'. Benton's work continues to be a most comprehensive and valued source of information for Essex historians today.

Benton was well-known during his lifetime, travelling the area and talking to local people in the course of his historical and archaeological researches.

Benton's mother died in January 1874, followed by his wife that May. He apparently consulted his children over the choice of a second wife and, in January 1876, married Elizabeth Warren, formerly the family's governess. The couple returned to live in North Shoebury House in 1886.

Benton's final home was Frankleigh House, Whitegate Road, Southend (now part of Southend High Street) where he died of heart failure on 23 March 1898. He was buried, according to his wishes, in the churchyard at Shopland with a funeral that attracted 'a large assembly of friends and neighbours' (*Southend Standard*).

98 Philip Benton, 1815-98. Benton wrote the *History of the Rochford Hundred*.

Fortunately, most of Benton's manuscripts, drawings and notes eventually came into the possession of the Essex Record Office.

Dale Knapping

One night in 1861, a fire broke out at South Shoebury Hall, then owned by Robert Bristow. Dozens (some reports cite hundreds) of soldiers from the garrison raced to assist, and began to move haystacks out of the path of the blaze. Another group of soldiers entered the house where they consumed many bottles of wine and liquor; door panels and windows were smashed; beds and furniture were broken. The scene the next morning saw Shoebury Common strewn with debris from the Hall. The few men found in possession of goods were imprisoned by a civil court, although most of the culprits were never identified.

Soon after this disaster it was found that Robert Bristow's extravagant lifestyle had depleted the family fortunes to an unsustainable extent. He left behind his role as lord of the manor of South Shoebury and moved to London to work as a taxi driver.

99   Gladys Cause and her daughter Emily outside their greengrocers at 40 High Street, *c.*1902.

However, Bristow's misfortune was Dale Knapping's opportunity and, in 1866, South Shoebury Hall was offered for sale by auction. It was described in the catalogue as 'a comfortable residence, containing on the ground floor, entrance hall, dining and drawing rooms, two sitting rooms in the rear, kitchen, scullery, dairy, larder and cellar; on the first floor, two good bedchambers and three other bedrooms at back, approached by a separate staircase, on the upper floor, two attics'. In addition, there was a six-roomed cottage, plus a stable, coach house, fowl house, two yards with a barn, cowshed, stabling, cart lodge and piggery. All these were new buildings, the originals having been destroyed in the 1861 fire.

Dale Knapping (1823-78), already the tenant farmer of both South Shoebury Hall Farm and Suttons Farm and rapidly making his fortune from the brickworks, was the purchaser of both of these properties. With his purchase he became the new, and the last, lord of the manor of South Shoebury.

Knapping's grandfather, John, was the youngest of 10 children born to Christopher Knapping, the tenant farmer at Shopland Hall. John became a lawyer, married Mary Dale and moved into Suttons, South Shoebury. His eldest son, Christopher Dale Knapping, took on the tenancy of South Shoebury Hall Farm and fathered two sons, William and Dale. William took over the farm while Dale became a JP and married Mary Asplin, a cousin of Christopher Parsons.

Knapping was respected for bringing much needed employment to the area and

100 James and Ellen Parker with children Dorothy and Wesley, pictured in 1907 outside their grocers and fruit shop.

is remembered as being benevolent to his employees and local people in general. For example, he bought back a small section of land from the government at the end of Rampart Street to allow public access onto East Beach. The public could then use the beach between George Street and Blackgate Road when there was no firing practice, as indicated by red flags flying. He was a generous benefactor to the new school in Hinguar Street and paid for the making up of Rampart Street and High Street.

Knapping died of a heart attack in 1878 while on one of his many visits to Paris, but was brought home and buried at St Andrew's. The *Southend Standard* said: 'His loss will be felt by all classes'.

Property Builds and Sales

Towards the end of the 19th century, when the garrison was an established feature of South Shoebury and Parsons, Benton and Knapping were old men, there was much exchange of property in both Shoebury parishes. The price of wheat was falling, largely due to the availability of cheap imports from America, and farmers struggled to make ends meet. Fewer sons wanted to follow their fathers into agriculture. Selling out to the brickfield owners or even the War Department made good financial sense. Property developers, too, were eager for land to build housing for the workers attracted by the new employment opportunities of the area.

101 The Wesleyan Methodist Church was built in the High Street in 1893.

Samuel Poynter jnr of Crouchmans Farm gave a speech to the Central Chamber of Agriculture in 1887 saying: 'Foreign competition is compelling farmers to sell under cost price and is ruining the English farmer.'

In 1897, Crouchmans was sold to Arthur Mills Kelmsley who built a market gardening nursery there. Market gardening became a viable option with the advent of the railway, enabling farmers to transport their perishable produce quickly to the London markets.

102 Methodist Society parade in the High Street, 1911.

Kelmsley donated money for the restoration of both St Mary's and Great Wakering church. Little Crouchmans was built in 1910 for his second daughter and her husband.

Henry Webb of Friends Farm died in 1872 and a portion of that farm was sold by his trustees in 1885 to land developer Frederic Ramuz (later mayor of Southend).

George Alp, son of William Alp of Rampart Farm and later Friars Farm, built a blacksmith's shop on the beach below Rampart Terrace in 1877 as a repair shop for the barges being built next door at Mr Cook's boathouse. *The Shoebury* barge, for example, built by Mr Rose for Mr Cook himself, could carry 50,000 bricks. During the heyday of the brickfields, six shipwrights were employed to build and repair boats and as many as five or six boats at a time would be hauled up onto the beach waiting to be worked on.

The blacksmith's shop burnt down after 20 years but was rebuilt and taken over by Mr Sawkins, who also worked on the barges. Demand was such that horses were having to wait up to two hours to be shod. George Alp became a builder and is responsible for many

103 A photograph taken of the parade in the High Street 'when the volunteers went away' in August 1905.

houses in old Shoebury village. Mr Rose took over the boat builders, together with his sons, who expanded the business to build pleasure craft, motor boats and bawleys for the Leigh cockle industry.

In 1877, the Rochford Rural Sanitary Authority directed the Inspector of Nuisances to send all cases of infectious diseases to Shoebury Hospital. Subsequently, in 1889, the clerk to the Authority was asked to 'find out to whom Shoebury Infectious Hospital belongs and what control this Authority has over it'. Unfortunately, the results of his enquiries were not recorded and it has been impossible to ascertain the location and nature of this hospital. Most likely, the 'hospital' was an isolated cottage, well away from any other residences.

However, this hospital was obsolete by 1901 when Shoebury Urban District Council joined with Rochford Rural District Council to rent out an isolation hospital at Hawkwell and later a cottage at Sutton Ford (East Street/Sutton Road junction, Southend). Thus, infectious persons from Shoebury would be loaded onto a wagon and driven over bumpy cart tracks to this little cottage.

The land and properties at Parsons Corner were sold by Mrs W. Knapping in December 1887. The sale included a grocer's shop with a 'keeping room', parlour and cellar, six freehold cottages, a blacksmith's shop and dwelling house, plus a brewhouse, stable, cart shed, small garden and a plot of freehold land. William Runacres was tenant of the grocers, while Charles Hawkins was the blacksmith. The properties shared the use of a well with a pump, the tenants paying towards its upkeep and repair. The purchaser paid £590 for the lot.

Local Concerns

Drownings were still a common event, although some were more unfortunate than others. Fisherman George Houghton fell out of his boat in December 1873; his friend, Alonzo Duer, found him too heavy to pull back into the boat, so he tied a rope to the drowning man's knee and rowed as fast as he could to Shoebury coastguard station. Needless to say, by the time he arrived, poor George was dead.

1 March 1874 saw another destructive high tide, when a 50ft-wide breach was made in

104   A carriage parade in the High Street on the occasion of the marriage of the daughter of Col J. Jocelyn, the Commandant, to Lt Strachan, 1907.

the Shoeburyness sea wall and 800 men from the garrison were called on to help. Shoebury Common was completely inundated and an immense number of wild rabbits lost their lives. One of the people most disheartened by this was probably Isaac Mulbank of Great Wakering who, four months earlier, was committed to two months' hard labour for trespassing on that same land in search of one or two rabbits for his cooking pot.

Fifty garrison officers volunteered to help repair a sea wall breach on Leigh Marsh and worked continuously for five hours. The *Southend Standard* reported: 'The value of the forces at Shoeburyness were thus proved in more than one instance.'

However, not all the garrison's members were equally public spirited. In July 1874, 20-30 members of the Royal Engineers caused a riot outside the *Minerva* on Southend seafront, when they insulted some ladies 'in a most disgraceful and unmanly manner' (*Southend Standard*). Fortunately, two policemen came along and the gang ran off, back to Shoebury.

Conversely, one month later, garrison men assisted Southend police when fighting broke out between groups of holidaymakers from the East End.

Eight
Parishes and Districts

Trades and services in South Shoebury continued to diversify with the increasing population. There were grocers, butchers, builders, drapers, a midwife and by 1900 a local physician, Walter Ernest. Shoeburyness, 'a point of land in this parish', and Cambridge Town were listed separately within the South Shoebury entry in Kelly's *Trade Directory*.

Cambridge Town

Before 1877 there was only one public house in the town, the *Shoebury Tavern*, where a gallon of beer cost 1s.

In 1877, a Mr Bradley built another public house in Ness Road to serve the expanding western side of the town, naming it the *Cambridge Hotel*, after the Duke of Cambridge. Initially, there was difficulty in obtaining a licence for

the pub as it was less than the statutory one mile from the *Shoebury Tavern*. However, Mr Outram, the manager, re-measured the distance via the Red Brick House and Danger Bridge and made it just over a mile. The licence was then granted and the hotel opened for business in 1879.

That year, *Shoebury Tavern* was taken over by William Kirkwood when his father, James, died. William laid on evening dances twice a week, decorating the gardens with coloured lights. The original building was demolished by the brewers in 1899 and replaced with the new *Shoebury Hotel*, built in the style of William Morris, with Mr Pontoon as the new landlord.

As soon as the *Cambridge Hotel* opened for business, residential development in this western part of the town took off, becoming known

105 *Shoeburyness Tavern*, High Street (in the early 1800s called *Rampart Tavern*). The inn was rebuilt in 1899 in the style of William Morris.

SHOEBURYNESS HOTEL
Proprietor : F. DESBOROUGH

This Hotel is complete with every comfort and patrons may rely on being well catered for

At the Shoebury Hotel you court all the best
You'll say so if put to the test.
Once you meet " Dessie " of the A.O.F.B.
You've caught his old smile with jo-vi-i-ty.

Lock-up Garages   Gymnasium   Billiard Saloon

Catering a Speciality
Seating Accommodation 125

This Hostelry is famous for its Gymnasium, greatly in favour with the boxing world. Here one may see the modern arrangements of the prize ring. Georges Carpentier, George Cook, Jack Bloomfield, Johnny Brown, Chas. Ledoux and many other champions made this their headquarters.

A Favourite Resort of Visitors and Pleasure Parties

R.A.O.B. Lodge   Telephone No. 5   Home from Home

106   *Shoeburyness Hotel* advertisement, c.1930.

107   *Cambridge Hotel* advertisement, c.1930.

108   *Cambridge Hotel*, Ness Road.

Cambridge Hotel
Shoeburyness
Few minutes walk from Beach

Mann Crossman & Paulin's
FAMOUS LONDON BEERS
IN EXCELLENT CONDITION

Spacious Lawn and Gardens
DANCING EVERY EVENING
IN LARGE HALL

Good Pull In for Motors

BEANFEASTS AND PARTIES CATERED FOR

Proprietor   -   -   A. E. INNELL

109   Hinguar Street School, *c.*1900.

as the Cambridge Estate or Cambridge Town. West Road was one of the first streets laid out with, at right angles to it, St Andrews Road, Seaview Road, Cambridge Road and Grove Road. These latter two now replaced with Avon Way, Chelmer Way, etc.

Seventy plots of land in Cambridge Road, Seaview Road and Grove Road were put up for auction by Albert Wells, a cocoa merchant of London, at the *Cambridge Hotel* in 1885. James Banyard purchased 61 of them for £744, paying £5 down, with the deeds of his bakery in the High Street as surety. Each plot measured approximately 20 feet by 90 feet and Banyard sold them off in ones and twos for about £20 per plot. Deeds of the plots stipulated that any building erected thereon was not to be used as a tavern, public house or beershop, nor were

any 'ashes or filth' to be stored on the plots, nor were any gypsies or tramps to be harboured or allowed to squat there.

West Road developed as the shopping area serving Cambridge Town. However, the population outstripped the provision of services and the first residents found themselves coping with unmade roads, no sewers or piped water. A local councillor described the area as 'a fever den', saying that the residents were 'living in a field without any system of roads, drains or water supply'.

In order to provide a public access road from this new estate to the village without having to use the public right of way through the garrison, a new road was laid out across the campfield in 1888-90. It was appropriately named Campfield Road, its layout following the existing field boundaries.

110 Hinguar Street School pupils, *c.*1905. The School Board asked the constable to deal with the nuisance of children, 'even respectable ones', chasing after motor vehicles that passed through the village. Children from North Shoebury were reprimanded when they stood on the wall near Great Wakering church and threw snowballs at passers-by.

Education

When in 1839 the London Diocesan Board of Education surveyed the educational provision in south-east Essex they found that the children of both North and South Shoebury attended Great Wakering school, built some 23 years earlier. Altogether about 73 children attended the school, paying 2d. each per week.

The first school in Shoebury itself was a single room erected in 1862 on the site of what is now St Peter's church, on Church Street, financed and built by Dale Knapping, George Smith and the Church of England. It included a schoolmaster's house and stables (now combined into a private home). With William Cox as the head teacher and his daughter, Eleanor, as assistant teacher, the building had space for 175 pupils and served as a chapel of ease for St Andrew's on Sundays. The Rev. Edward Cooper Wills, then curate but later vicar of South Shoebury, conducted morning services there. From 1872 until his death in 1892, the Rev. F. Thackeray, the vicar of Shopland and cousin of author William Thackeray, walked over from Shopland each Sunday to take evening service and then walked home again.

Children in North Shoebury continued to attend Great Wakering school.

Foster's Education Act of 1870 made elementary education compulsory and parishes were required to make school places available for all children. At South Shoebury, Hinguar

Street school (St Peter's site) fulfilled the requirements until the 1880s when a School Board of five members, officially instituted on 30 January 1885, was elected to raising funds for the building of a new school. A Board School accommodating 370 children was duly erected a few yards east of the existing school in 1886. Miss Jessie Grater was the first schoolmistress.

Discussions on enlarging the school were on-going from the early 1890s. Mr Glasscock wanted to extend the current building, while Mr Hayes and Mr Brooks favoured establishing a separate school on the Cambridge Estate. Mr Glasscock said that land on the Cambridge Estate would always be cheap and available – the School Board could purchase enough for a school when the need arrived, but Mr Brooks was concerned. 'I shall consider it my duty to inform the Education Department that children

are running about without anywhere to go,' he said. Initially, however, Mr Glasscock got his way and the Hinguar Street school buildings were enlarged in 1897.

The School Board discussed the fact that some 12 to 14 children left school at 11.30am each day to carry dinner to their fathers working on the brickfields. It was agreed to let the practice continue, although some members of the Board had their reservations.

In July 1894, Mr Bearman requested that the School Board allow his 11-year-old son to leave school in order to work on a local farm. The Chairman, Mr Harris, thought he would need a special certificate from the inspector because the by-laws of Shoebury required children to attend school until they had completed the Fifth Standard. Mr Brooks said he would just take the child out of school if it were him.

111 Shoebury railway station, built in 1883. As late as 1960, the railway line divided two different worlds – dense housing to the south and completely undeveloped agricultural land to the north.

112   Whent's stores and post office, on the corner of Seaview Road and West Road, sold everything from meat and groceries to hardware and tools.

'What encouragement is it to a working man to send his boy to school?', he asked.

Mr Bearman said he could not afford to keep his boy at school; nor could other members of the parish, who had sons of 10 years old working in the fields.

Railway

The London-Tilbury-Southend railway line reached Southend in 1854. At first, the army resisted any moves to extend it east, lest it compromised the security of their camp. However, the alternatives were water transport – for which a barge pier was constructed on the Ness in 1859 – or overland transport on roads that were little more than cart tracks. Both were sometimes restricted by weather conditions.

Therefore, in 1882, the War Office finally agreed to the extension of the railway line, an Act of Parliament gave formal permission for the extension, and Kirk and Parry were contracted to carry out the work. Cottages were built in Hinguar Street to house the workers, although this street and the adjoining Church Street were not made up until 1886. It was originally intended that Church Street should be extended north, parallel to the High Street. However, the laying of the railway foiled that plan and the road became part of Hinguar Street.

Work on the railway line began in 1883 and Brampton House, built in the High Street in 1867, was demolished with its neighbouring homes to make way for the single-storey weather-boarded station.

Eventually, the line to Shoebury opened on Friday, 1 February 1884, the first train being the 7.15am from Southend. A local journalist described the line as 'one of the most unexciting pieces of railway imaginable'. The countryside between Southend and Shoebury was, he said, 'almost empty'. However, two days later, 1,200 tickets were sold to passengers eager to make use of this section of the line.

The first stationmaster was Charles Beeton, with Mr King as his signalman; Messrs Kirby and Crowhurst were employed as porters. Until a shed was built at Shoebury, the first train was always the 7.15am from Southend, which formed the first 'up' train to London. It carried freight and passengers, used by both businesses and holidaymakers. The train journey from Southend cost 4d. for a return and took eight minutes.

Some of those who benefited most were the farmers who had seen the price of wheat fall dramatically in the 1870s. The railway allowed them to market more perishable produce in London and influenced the rise of dairy farming and market gardening.

In 1888, the War Department laid down their own permanent railway from the piers at the Ness, and dispensed with the services of horses which had previously been their only means of dragging heavy guns about on army land. A level crossing was laid across the High Street to join their tracks to the main railway line.

Church Developments

The new vicar of St Mary's, the Rev. Henry Wilmot, raised a mortgage on the glebe lands in 1883 to enable him to rebuild North Shoebury vicarage. Mrs Wilmot laid a new foundation stone in December of that year, beneath which were buried a jar containing a record of the proceedings, a newspaper dated

113 Wesleyan Church choir, 1907.

114   The garrison theatre, with a production of 'In a Persian Garden', June 1920. The iron-framed building arrived in sections via the railway in September 1884 and was assembled at the garrison gate for use as a theatre. It stood until 1954 when it was destroyed by arson.

7 December 1883 and some coins. The value of the living at this time was about £185 per annum. The great tithes, still entailed on the owners of North Shoebury House (at that time Major Onslow), were valued at £400 per annum.

The Rev. Wilmot also oversaw extensive restoration of St Mary's church in 1884-5, with the assistance of three members of the Benton family: Philip senior, Philip junior (the then churchwarden) and his brother, William, who was a professional architect. The stone floors were laid with tessellated wooden flooring, varnished deal pews were installed, the gallery was removed and the beams were denuded of their whitewash. The lancet windows of the chancel were opened out and an old wooden

window on the south of the nave was replaced with a 14th-century stone window; all the other windows were reglazed. A new lectern, pulpit and altar rails were provided.

In 1883, a Salvation Army hall opened in Ness Road. A Wesleyan Chapel was built in 1893 in the High Street with accommodation for 250 people, at a cost of £1,000. Fr. Callaghan came to assist old Fr Moore at St George's Catholic church in 1889. However, Shoeburyness did not get a resident Catholic priest until 1908 when Fr. Ingle was appointed.

Garrison Developments

The 1880s brought both highlights and disasters for the garrison. In 1884 a theatre was built near the gate, giving many years of pleasure to

115 Interior of garrison church, c.1960. This décor owes much to the Rev. Malim (chaplain 1884-93) who raised funds to beautify the church and declared it to be 'one of the prettiest in the country'. However, some of the more gaudy decoration was removed in about 1920.

soldier and civilian alike before it was destroyed by arson in 1954.

In February 1885, a tragic event made the national press when seven men, including the Commandant and Superintendent of Experiments, Colonel Fox-Strangways, died. A fuse was detonated prematurely while being prepared for use; flames and fragments flew out horizontally, ripping into bodies. Four doctors were immediately called. However, Gunner Underwood died instantly, followed by Captain Goold-Adams in the arms of his wife, Evelyn. Fox-Strangways, who had insisted that the other men were attended to first, Colonel Lyon, Gunner Daykin, Gunner Allen and Frederick Rance, a visitor from Woowich, all underwent leg amputations but later died.

Queen Victoria sent personal messages of sympathy to the widows and the garrison. The funerals, four of which were held at St Andrew's, attracted hundreds of mourners. Public subscription in memory of those killed paid for a new 'families' hospital in Campfield Road in 1898 (converted into the *Captain Mannering* pub in the 1980s).

More happily, the garrison initiated the first Shoebury Week in 1885: seven days of concerts and games, plus theatricals, dances, treasure hunts, gymkhana, cricket matches and a grand ball.

When in 1888 longer ranges were deemed necessary to test the increasingly large guns, the War Department purchased much of Friends Farm from Frederic Ramuz, plus 127 acres of

Barnfleet Farm. This area north of Blackgate Road, extending to Foulness, became known as the New Ranges, the first trials being held there in 1890, while the Old Ranges remained in use for accommodation and education only. The total military area was 580 acres by April 1893.

Chapman's House, rebuilt in 1868, was purchased from Knapping's daughters for £25,000 and became absorbed into the New Ranges as offices. The stables, coach house and cart sheds of Suttons were now used as gun sheds and stores, while the Royal Engineers took over Cherrytree Farm farmhouse as their offices. Some fields of Cherrytree Farm became part of New Friars Farm, for which a new farmhouse was built north of Elm Road.

Wakering Road was built in 1891, and the old road running past Suttons house became

exclusive to the military. The Officers' Mess was reconstructed in 1898; all but a small portion of the old coastguard station was demolished and replaced with a new Single Officers Quarters. More married quarters were built in Campfield Road in 1899, known as Bird Cage quarters because of their railings.

The firing of the guns, by now a fact of life at Shoebury, was occasionally known to cause broken windows and even the collapse of ceilings. New rifled weapons designed by Messrs Armstrong made their debut at the experimental establishment and revolutionised the art of gunnery.

Shoebury Urban District Council

The 1894 Local Government Act allowed the establishment of Rural Districts and Parish

116 New Range Avenue. The military began purchasing land along the North Shoebury coast, including Suttons, Chapmans, Cherrytree, Barnfleet and Friends Farms, from 1888. The area, together with Foulness, became known as the New Ranges.

117 Shoeburyness Urban District Council, *c.*1930. Fred Cause, centre front, was Chairman of the Council. The council offices, built in 1910, are now the police station.

Councils, and a public meeting debated whether North and South Shoebury should apply to become amalgamated into a single government district. However, the initial vote was against this and the ratepayers of South Shoebury applied to the County Council to be constituted as a local government district by themselves. A meeting led by a Parliamentary Committee of the County Council chaired by Councillor W. Lloyd Wise and about 40 Shoebury ratepayers was held in May 1894 at Shoebury schoolroom to discuss the proposals.

Frederic Gregson, on behalf of the promoters of the movement, said that the population of Shoeburyness had numbered 1,274 in 1881 but had grown to 1,986 in 1891, with an additional 1,000 members of the military and their families. The parish had about 440 houses and a total size of 1,010 acres, including no more than 300 acres of rural land. It was mostly 'accommodation land'.

Mr Cox, Assistant Overseer and Collector of Rates, said the rateable value of South Shoebury, exclusive of the War Department's £2,200 paid in lieu of rates, was £7,759 10s.

– of this £6,861 was upon houses and £898 on land. This showed how far South Shoebury had come from the agricultural parish it had been only 50 years previously. There had been about 80 houses built in the parish during the last three years.

Mr Gregson thought that South Shoebury should have the power to make the place fit for its many summer visitors and the soldiers

118 A new electricity supply to Shoeburyness is switched on by Cllr Boosey, Chairman of the Council, *c.*1920.

119   High Street and *Shoeburyness Hotel*, *c.*1920. Between the hotel and the garrison is Jenkins garage, which later moved to a site near the station.

billeted there, something they could not do under the present system of government.

Furthermore, he said, Shoebury was under the Rochford Rural Sanitary Authority which met at Rochford seven miles away; the medical officer lived at Southend and the Nuisance

120   Café, Shoeburyness promenade, *c.*1930. Immediately beyond the café was the brickworks.

Inspector at Rayleigh. In the case of infectious diseases, they had to telegraph to Rayleigh and wait two days for an ambulance. Alternatively, they had to send to Southend for the Medical Officer of Health, wait for him and then, upon his advice, send to Rayleigh for Mr Judd, who had to find out whether there was accommodation at the hospital and then send to Shoebury for the patient. Mr Glasscock, a resident of 38 years, said it usually took three days to get a patient away.

The Sanitary Authority had no power to deal with the making up of new streets, so the new roads existing in or near the Cambridge Estate which were unmade remained unmade and were described as being 'nothing but filth and dirt'. Under the existing system, each property holder was responsible for his own stretch of road, leading to situations where one man made

121 Cambridge Town Boys Band.

his part of the road six inches higher than that of his neighbour.

Mr Gregson said the parish should have leave to manage its own affairs, such as developing the water scheme. Furthermore, he did not know of a single landowner or ratepayer, including the military, who was opposed to the idea of a District Council.

Following this meeting, and due deliberation by the County Council, permission for an urban district was duly granted, much to the delight of the residents.

George Glasscock was elected chairman and the first meeting was held on 2 January 1895 with nine council members. One of their first decisions was announced in the *Southend Standard* that week:

Notice is hereby given that pursuant to a Resolution of the SOUTH SHOEBURY URBAN DISTRICT COUNCIL and with the sanction of the ESSEX COUNTY COUNCIL acting by the District and Parish Councils committee of such Council, the South Shoebury Urban District will henceforth be called and known as the SHOEBURYNESS URBAN DISTRICT and the Council of the District will henceforth be called and known as the SHOEBURYNESS URBAN DISTRICT COUNCIL.

By order of the District Council.

Frederic Gregson, clerk. 11th January 1895.

The Council met fortnightly on Tuesday nights at 7.30pm in the schoolroom. Their first year saw oil street lamps installed in Cambridge Town, the first water mains laid and an Inspector of Nuisances employed on a salary of £25 p.a.

The residents of North Shoebury, because of the small size of the parish, decided to remain as part of Rochford Rural District. The first

122   East Beach. The barge in the background was one of two owned by the War Department and used for positioning targets out at sea.

meeting of the new Rochford Rural District Council was on 1 January 1895 with 26 members representing the parishes, including James Hutley of North Shoebury Hall. North Shoebury itself decided that even a formal parish council was unnecessary and agreed to hold annual parish meetings, with special meetings called when required. Their first parish meeting (as opposed to the former vestry meetings) was held on 4 December 1894, at which the vicar, the Rev. Wilmot, was elected chairman and Mr Dickson the secretary. Subsequent meetings were held at North Shoebury Hall, usually on a Wednesday evening and, after 1898, in the new parish room, which had been financed by public subscription and built of corrugated iron on timber framing north-west of the church in 1897.

Flooding

Despite these new developments, Nature continued as she had for centuries. On 19 November 1897, gale force winds and a high tide caused massive flooding, especially on the North Shoebury coast as well as damaging towns and villages from Canvey Island to Walton-on-the-Naze. According to the *Essex Chronicle*, Foulness was 'inundated', while Great Wakering was 'badly flooded' and 10 soldiers from the Shoeburyness barracks were swept away in their two boats, ending up in Kent.

That week, children living on the Cambridge Estate had to be taken to school by cart as the roads were impassable on foot. In addition, several elderly people were unable to attend the annual 'old folks and widows' tea provided at St Andrew's hall. The *Southend Standard* noted: 'Great distress is prevailing amongst the working classes [at Shoeburyness] on account of the severe weather, which prevents the men from following their usual employment.'

Southend Borough had absorbed Southchurch parish in 1897; housing development was slowly creeping eastwards towards Shoebury.

Nine

A New Century

By 1901, the population of North Shoebury was 205 – little increase in 100 years. In contrast, the population of Shoeburyness Urban District was 2,990, including 988 men quartered at the garrison. That year, Shoebury Avenue, Wakering Avenue, Southchurch Avenue, Friars Street and Wallace Street were built off the High Street, while, in Cambridge Town, Trafalgar Road, Caulfield Road, Waterloo Road and Richmond Avenue were made up.

When Shoebury Cottage and its grounds in the extreme south-west of the parish were developed, the streets were named after Ynyr Burges' native Ireland, e.g. Connaught, Leitrim, Ulster, and so on.

Not everyone was pleased with the new developments, however, and in 1905 Mr Childs of Richmond Avenue had the bath removed from his house to reduce his rates bill. The Seabourne Estate was developed in 1911, with 58 plots in Church Road, St Andrew's Road and Richmond Avenue. Most of Shoebury's roads were made up by 1914.

A fire service was formed in 1905, led by Captain S. Munday with Mr Hatcher and Fred Cause as 2nd and 3rd officers, using premises at the back of an off-licence in West Road as a fire station. The council provided a ladder, a hose and a handcart. Three years later, the brigade moved their headquarters to Talmage's yard in

123 West Road. In 1893, garrison commandant Colonel Richardson said that he had never been in a place where such insanitary conditions existed as at Shoebury.

124   Linton Road. When Linton Road was first made-up, old pots and pans were incorporated into the hard-core and a council meeting in 1903 heard that the houses were 'the rottenest in Shoebury' and in danger of falling down.

125   Shoeburyness Fire Brigade, pictured soon after its formation in 1905.

126 Richmond Avenue School, c.1905. The town's first library was at this school, until a branch library opened in Ness Road in 1945.

Shoebury Avenue where they paid 2s. 6d. rent. They moved into permanent premises when new chambers for Shoeburyness Council were built at the junction of Shoebury Avenue and High Street in 1910 at a cost of £828.

On Friday, 5 May 1905, crowds gathered on Shoebury beach to watch tug boats from Sheerness work to refloat the armoured cruiser HMS *King Alfred*, beached on the sandbanks. The ship was eventually able to continue her journey three days later.

The artillery had been split into the Royal Field Artillery and the Royal Garrison Artillery, with Shoeburyness now involved with the latter and concentrating on naval weapons. The School of Gunnery and the Experimental Establishment became separate entities in 1905. By 1918 the whole of Foulness, except the church, rectory, mission hall and school, belonged to the War Department, although the road and bridges were not completed until 1924.

New schools

In February 1904 James Brooks got his wish for a school on the Cambridge Estate and 60 children transferred to a new infant school building at Richmond Avenue under the guardianship of Miss E. Golding, Miss Orbell and Miss Brooks. The inspectors reported later that year, 'The infants are, on the whole, well managed and carefully employed'. The new school could accommodate 200 children, although initially attendance averaged 140 pupils.

That same year, a junior block was added to Hinguar Street school. Mr Cox, the headmaster, was followed by Mr Hillyer, Mr Deal and then Mr Dale. The original building (St Peter's site) continued as part of the school until 1911 when it became a hall for the first St Peter's Church.

The school log book records repeated cases of measles, chicken pox, mumps and whooping cough, with up to 60 children absent at a time.

127   Richmond Avenue school group, *c.*1905.

128   Headmistress Miss Cardinal with the staff of Richmond Avenue school.

129   Richmond Avenue, *c.*1915. When Richmond Avenue was built up, the houses backed on to open land stretching as far as Thorpe Bay Broadway.

Poor weather, too, was the cause of much absenteeism: 'A bad attendance, caused by a wet, rough morning', 'A great many children away this afternoon on account of the wind and rain', 'A heavy rain caused a bad attendance'.

Despite these distractions to education, the inspector recorded in 1911 that 'the children are bright and quiet and much of the work reaches a high standard'. The children enjoyed half-days off school to visit the annual Shoebury fête, the garrison sports day and the Sunday School treat.

In 1910 the annual report by the County Medical Officer, Dr John Thresh, confirmed that Shoeburyness had the highest birth rate in Essex.

Urban Developments

An extension of Southend Council's tramway system to Shoebury was hotly debated, with most Shoebury residents in favour of the scheme.

The 600 new homes on the Cambridge Estate and up to 400 people walking from Southend to Shoeburyness every day during holiday season were cited as reasons for a tram service.

1907 saw the first Southend to Shoebury bus service and in 1909 a new barge pier was built, but the tramway extension had not even begun when the whole network was abandoned as being financially unviable.

St Mary's church spire was restored in 1911 and this, together with the Coronation of King George V, was honoured with a special church service followed by a procession of school children to the vicarage garden for tea and a souvenir coronation mug.

The North Shoebury parish meeting expressed its sympathy to Mrs Hutley on the death of her husband, James, in March 1912. He had lived at North Shoebury Hall since 1891 and had served as parish overseer for many years, representing the parish on the Rochford

130   Hinguar Street pupils, c.1925. The headmistress of Hinguar School reported in May 1918: '… this year has been a very trying one to scholars and teachers alike; the frequent air raids … have caused adverse conditions to progress.'

131   St Peter's Church choir football club, 1907. Mr Giles with, back: Walter Giles, Arthur Dray, Frank Mott. Middle: William Bradshaw, Harold Johnson, Ralph Mott. Front: Robert Watkins, Jarratt Leaney, Harold Franks, Albert Rayner, Albert Walters.

Rural District Council. Parishioners described him as 'of the most kindly disposition and of very hospitable nature'.

A special meeting of North Shoebury parish was held in July 1912 to protest that the War Office had placed 'barbed wire entanglements' over the seawall between Wakering Stairs and Shoebury boundary, obstructing the right of way. A similar meeting the following year considered the War Department's proposal to replace the Broomway with a road and bridges to Foulness. All present opposed the idea and agreed to send three delegates to speak against the proposals. However, the War Department had their own complaints against locals; for example, an important plating trial before a party of senior officials in 1912 was delayed by a man driving a pig down the Broomway.

132 The Palace Theatre, Ness Road, opened on 10 May 1913 with seating for 500, and closed on 5 March 1955.

133 Palace Theatre and war memorial, c.1921.

134   Victory celebration parade, 1918.

Other matters concerning North Shoebury parish were the general bad state of repair of the roads, including frequent flooding at Parsons Corner, caused by the ancient ditches being replaced by inadequate pipes. The rateable value of North Shoebury was £130 and that of South Shoebury exactly twice that.

A cinema named the Palace Theatre opened on the corner of Ness Road and Campfield Road on 10 May 1913 with seating for 500 patrons in stalls and a balcony. By 1929 it had become known simply as The Palace, or locally as the Bug Hutch, and was modernised during the 1930s under the new ownership of the London and Provincial Cinemas Ltd, at which time the accommodation was reduced to 360 seats. It closed on 5 March 1955 when it was under the ownership of Mr L. Griffin.

Subsequently, the building came into use as a camping supplies shop.

First World War

Winston Churchill visited Shoeburyness in 1912, in his capacity as First Lord of the Admiralty.

1914 saw Shoeburyness once again in the frontline of defence of England and garrison numbers rose from four officers and 80 men in 1914 to 17 officers, 341 men and 80 civilian staff in 1918.

Hundreds of soldiers found themselves in Shoebury – some billeted temporarily on their way to France, others for training. Local homes and the schoolroom were used as billets, and Shoebury remained on active alert. Married families had to leave their quarters on the garrison to make way for troops on active service. The theatre was taken

135   Capt. H. Goodwin, Instructor RA (centre front) with men on the 70th Officers' Course, 4 September 1918.

over as an emergency hospital with 40 beds but, undeterred, the soldiers moved the entertainments to the drill shed. The Commandant's house became an officers' mess, with a branch mess at the *Shoebury Hotel*. Training expanded into anti-aircraft instruction and war dog school. With the influx of so many young men, inter-regimental fights were not unknown.

George V visited the New Ranges on 4 April 1916 to witness the testing of a variety of equipment. He took lunch in the officers' mess and inspected the School of Gunnery. Local school children lined up in Motts Meadow (off the High Street) to watch the king and his entourage pass by.

Despite heavy bombing in the Rochford Hundred, the garrison escaped the war unscathed by bombs. In fact, the greatest catastrophe occurred in 1918 when some workers allowed a fire to run out of control on the New Ranges. Flames spread to ammunition dumps nearby and for 24 hours explosions rent the air as the fire leapt from store to dump to trucks loaded with ammunition. General panic ensued. The whole village was called to evacuate and a sergeant rode down the street calling 'Everybody out!' A refugee centre was set up at the Kursaal for those walking along the seafront from Shoebury with nowhere else to go. One man and some horses lost their lives, and £3 million of essential equipment was lost.

In 1919 the vicar of North Shoebury, the Rev. Morgan, suggested that a tablet be erected in St Mary's as a war memorial. In Shoeburyness, on 25 June 1920, a 40ft flagstaff and mahogany plaque was unveiled at Hinguar Street School detailing the names of 46 former pupils and masters who, out of the 310 old boys who had served in the forces, did not return.

The following year Colonel P. Holbrook unveiled the town's official war memorial at the junction of Ness and Campfield Roads. The Portland Stone monument, paid for by public subscriptions and fund raising events, was 18 feet high with eight tablets bearing the names of 85 fallen heroes at its base. Fifty members of the garrison acted as a guard of honour at the dedication service led by the Rev. G. Ellis-Jones of St Andrew's. In all, 640 Shoeburyness men had seen active service. The memorial was moved to Campfield Road in 1938.

Inter-War Development

After the First World War, farming was an increasingly unpopular occupation as costs rose and prices fell. There was less work for brickworkers or builders and Fred Cause and his wife set up a soup kitchen, where children would take jugs to be filled when there was no food to be had in the house.

Several women supplemented their incomes by taking in washing from the garrison. They could make one shilling for a bundle of a shirt, vest, one pair of pants, a pair of socks and a towel.

Incoming barges were closely watched by the villagers – lumps of coal that fell from wheelbarrows bringing material ashore along narrow planks were fair pickings. The brickfields continued to prosper during the 1920s and barge owners could charge £8-£9 per trip to London with a full load of bricks. This money was shared equally between the boat owner and the crew, with the crew's share being divided again, two-thirds to the skipper and one third to the mate.

136   War memorial, Ness Road.

137   No.2 Battery DRGA, who won the Kings Prize in 1921 at Shoebury's annual National Artillery competition.

138   Ladies Bowling team, *c.*1940.

139   Hinguar Street school pupils, *c.*1920.

September 1919 saw the sale of the 17-acre New Farm (which had replaced the former Doors Farm) for £2,700. That same month, White House Farm on what is now Bournes Green Chase, including some 42 acres of land and then run as a market garden, was sold to development company Southend Estates Co. Ltd for £7,650.

In these hard times entertainment was warmly welcomed and in 1919 the garrison theatre, much missed during the war, was restored with an orchestra pit and lampshades made for the band out of Cerebos salt tins.

Mr Desborough retired as Officers' Mess Steward and took over the *Shoeburyness Hotel* where he converted a back room for boxing training. Georges Carpentier (World Heavyweight Champion), Paul Fritsch (European Bantamweight Champion) and Bombardier Billy

Wells were just three of those who trained there. Boxing was also popular at a boys' club set up by the garrison. Regular dances and balls were held in the officers' mess, often with more than 200 guests. Shoebury Week festivities, suspended during the war, began again in 1921.

The original school building was dedicated as the new St Peter's church in 1920. The first St Peter's, an iron building erected in Dane Street in 1899, was wheeled on rollers to become the new church hall. When the hall became unsafe after the 1987 hurricane, the site was sold for flats and a new hall was built.

The horse and field elements of the School of Gunnery relocated to Salisbury Plain in 1920, while the newly named Coast Artillery School remained at Shoeburyness until 1940 when it moved to North Wales. During the 1920s the garrison reduced in size with Campfield Road and part of Chapel Road becoming public. A new west gate was created in Chapel Road with 101 Campfield Road, built in 1934, as the gatehouse.

The War Department again fell out of favour with North Shoebury and the parish meeting heard that the gates that used to stand at the entrance to the old road leading to Suttons were removed in April 1922 and placed across the main road at Cupid's Corner, obstructing the right of way to Friends Farm.

At this time the residents again discussed setting up a formal parish council for North Shoebury, but the feeling was that the informal meetings were advantageous in such a small parish and Mr Tillbrook proposed 'we go on as we are'. In 1923, still without a complete sewerage system, the parish asked Rochford Rural District Council to employ a 'scavenger' to collect refuse and lavatory pails. However, in 1927 they requested that the service be discontinued as it was too costly and the residents went back to dealing with their own lavatory pails. At least the parish had secured a reliable water supply, having negotiated a service from the Southend Water Company in 1924.

While demand for housing in North Shoebury was minimal, residential development continued apace in Shoeburyness, and Thorpedene Gardens, Tudor Gardens and Vincent Gardens (named

140   Beach huts at East Beach. The 1931 town guide suggested that 'for the tired and jaded city worker, there can be no better tonic than the invigorating and bracing air that greets him as he alights from the train at Shoebury'.

141   Uncle Tom's Cabin, *c.*1930. The Medical Officer for Health reported in 1929 that '… it may truly be said that Shoeburyness is one of the healthiest Seaside Resorts in England'.

after Councillor R. Vincent Cook) were built during 1924. In 1926 James Banyard developed the Bridge House Estate, in partnership with Sylvester Levett of Crouchmans.

In April 1923 Miss A. Banning was the first female elected to Shoebury District Council. Village GP Dr Paddy Ryan became civilian practitioner for the garrison and was much respected by all.

Most of the local railway workers were out during the 1926 General Strike, and held frequent meetings near the cinema. Garrison troops were deployed to guard various public utilities.

Population increase (over 35,000 by 1925) necessitated another extension to Richmond Avenue School in 1928, bringing the total to 520 scholars. Despite this, the Wesleyan Church Hall in the High Street was rented out for at least three years at £2 per week to provide additional accommodation for Hinguar Street School.

A Holiday Resort

As early as 1907, Shoeburyness Council had discussed proposals to change the village name to Shoeburyness-on-Sea to boost its appeal as a holiday resort. The decision eventually went against this idea.

During the 1930s there were plans to develop East Beach as a resort, but delay and then the war meant that this never materialised. However, a small holiday camp, with caravans and tents, was set up to the south of South Shoebury Hall.

As well as the increasing numbers of holidaymakers, the 1931 *Official Guide* to Shoeburyness noted that increasing numbers of city workers were making their homes in Shoebury. It advised that 'for the tired and jaded city worker, there can be no better tonic than the invigorating and bracing air that greets him as he alights from the train at Shoebury'. Another advantage of the town was the 'many countryside walks close at hand' – this referred to the still rural North Shoebury, described as 'a charming cluster of farms'. Elm Road was 'a pleasant lane' while Campfield Road was 'a peaceful lane running between fields'.

West Road, however, was becoming a bustling shopping area with milk churns arriving daily on a cart, an ice cream seller on a tricycle, a muffin man and a shrimp seller.

Ness Road was widened in 1930, involving the demolition of the building standing on the site of the original Well House. Other improvements instigated by the District Council were the erection of public and private bathing huts on the seafront, a designated car parking area and refreshment kiosk.

In 1931 North Shoebury held a meeting to discuss whether the parish should become a part of Shoeburyness Urban District and a part of Southend Borough. The major concern against the proposals was fear of an increase in rates. Major A. Wedd, the parish's representative at Essex County Council, recommended a formal

142   West Road. Land west of here was purchased by the Burges estate and roads such as Connaught, Cranley, Ulster and Stroma Gardens were named after Ynry Burges' native Ireland.

meeting between all the parishes to obtain more information.

Southend Borough

The expanding borough of Southend was finally successful in 1933 in annexing South Shoebury and most of North Shoebury. Shoeburyness Urban District Council ceased to exist on 30 September 1933, and the area came under the jurisdiction of the Borough of Southend from 1 October. Of the union with Southend, local councillors and tradesmen said that Southend should hang out the flags to celebrate its good fortune. Shoebury, they said, is the 'front door' of Southend and the union 'would allow the borough to develop a seaside resort that would be second to none in the country'.

From the same date, 1 October 1933, the north-eastern section of North Shoebury, including Crouchmans and Friends Farms and the new Seaview Estate (Seaview Drive, Goldsworthy Drive, and so on) became part of Great Wakering, governed by Rochford Urban District Council.

Southend Council immediately proceeded with additional development of the Thorpedene Estate. The Elm Road recreation ground opened in 1933, providing six acres of public space.

A police inspector was appointed to the Shoebury section and accommodated at 'Monville' in Thorpedene Gardens, where the front room was used as a police office. A new police station and cottages at Elm Road opened in March 1935. Shoebury's fire station became a sub-station of Southend.

Dale Knapping's youngest daughter, Margaret, died in 1935, at which time the lordship of the manor of South Shoebury reverted to the Crown.

The population growth was such that plans for a separate high school building were approved in 1938, and The Shoebury Senior School, costing about £35,500, opened in Caulfield Road in 1939. Mr F. Dale transferred from Hinguar Street to become the first headmaster.

However, the steady development of Shoebury was once again interrupted by war.

Ten

Towards a New Millennium

Second World War

On 1 June 1939, Ewen Bowyer took up his post as headmaster of Hinguar Street School. His tenure proved to be completely different from his previous teaching experience. Following the declaration of war, the school did not reopen after the summer break until 9 January 1940 and, on 26 May 1940, it was announced that all children in east-coast towns were to be evacuated inland for their own safety. A parents' meeting was held at the school on 28 May and, just five days later at 8.00am, 164 children and their teachers left the school for Chapel-en-le-Frith in Derbyshire. For some children this may have been traumatic, for others an adventure, but spare a thought for the mothers left weeping at the roadside as their children were driven away.

On arrival in Derbyshire the children from Shoebury were divided into four groups and taken to the villages of Edale, Castleton, Hope and Bamford, where they were 'distributed to private billets'. Mr Bowyer remained in Derbyshire co-ordinating the education of the children.

In the pupils' absence, both Hinguar Street and Richmond Avenue School buildings were requisitioned by the military. Armed forces also took over the Sunshine Home hospital building in Ness Road, while officers occupied Suttons. After the war Suttons' staircase and oak panelling were removed from the house apparently damaged – but not by enemy action.

Hundreds of militiamen and gunner reservists arrived for training. 22 Regiment included Gunner Frank Howard who became fully involved in concert parties and was remembered by one sergeant-major as being capable of transforming 'an entire parade into a lunatic asylum'. As Frankie Howerd he went on to become one of Britain's best loved comedians.

Shoebury garrison was armed with a battery of 6-inch naval guns to protect against seaborne invasion. Set in concrete casements, these guns had a range of seven miles across the estuary. They were controlled from a Battery Observation post and, for night-time illumination of enemy warships trying to slip up the river, they were twinned with coastal artillery searchlights in bunkers on the flanks of the battery. In average visibility the lights had a range of two miles.

Along the estuary coast, an almost continuous chain of 5ft by 5ft, 7ft-high anti-tank blocks lined the promenade. Anti-tank 'pimples' were set on Shoebury Common, backed by defensive scaffolding.

A wooden boom, nearly three miles long, was built out into the North Sea from East Beach to control shipping. An identical boom extended from the Kent shore, joined to the Shoebury boom by a net suspended from buoys. This centre section could be opened by tugboats to allow access to allied ships. It proved a successful defence, even against a German E-boat, which attempted to 'jump' the boom. The boom was retained after the war and even strengthened with stone to play its part in the Cold War against the Soviet Bloc. Further out, concrete forts were built.

In the run-up to D-Day, all ranks had to remain fully armed during working hours

143 High Street, c.1915. During the 1920s, local dairyman Mr Murray would walk the streets with milk churns on his handcart, dispensing milk into the jugs and basins people brought out.

and 20 ATS girls arrived to assist with the experimental trials.

Intense air activity in 1940 led to the garrison training school being moved to

144 High Street at its junction with Southchurch Avenue, looking south.

Llandudno. Others were not easily deterred and the Rev. Fitzpatrick insisted on his congregation finishing the hymn despite the air raids. Nicknamed the Galloping Major, he was known for riding a large horse around the barracks. Similarly, the garrison vs Essex Regiment cricket match was only abandoned when the nosecap of an AA shell fell on the pavilion roof.

The North and South Shoebury detachments of the Local Defence Volunteers were formed in June 1940, Sections 6 and 7 of 2 platoon (Southend East). Thorpe Bay golf course became a convenient practice area.

In August 1940, 31 bombs were jettisoned over Shoebury by German planes returning home. A married couple in West Road and a railway signalman died. Altogether, about 300

145 VE Day street party at Herbert Road, 7 May 1945.

tons of bombs were tipped on the foreshore east of Shoebury by bombers on their way back to Germany, but most fell on Foulness, New Ranges or the sands. Several enemy aircraft made forced landings that summer including, on 23 August, a Messerschmit 109 near the officers' mess – its pilot was quickly arrested.

Prime Minister Winston Churchill revisited the garrison in January and June 1941, and possibly on other occasions, to watch demonstrations.

It was perhaps with relief that Ewen Bowyer recorded in the Hinguar Street logbook on 31 August 1943: 'After three years and three months with evacuation parties in North Derbyshire, E.S. Bowyer resumed duty as headmaster of this school'. On the other hand, perhaps that relief was short-lived when up to

146 Advertisement of house builder, W. Allan, c.1930.

three air-raid warnings a day disrupted lessons during much of 1944-5 and shelter drill became a regular part of school life.

In May 1945, Mr Bowyer returned to Derbyshire to collect the remaining evacuees and on 6 June 1946 the children held a thanksgiving service, followed by a fancy dress parade and sports.

From August 1945, military personnel at the garrison were gradually depleted. The Experimental Establishment became the Proof and Experimental Establishment in 1948.

Of the fatalities suffered in Shoebury and Great Wakering during the war, fewer than half were due to enemy action. For example, minefields on the New Ranges killed four military personnel and two civilians, including a 13-year-old boy. In 1942, small parachute bombs released by the RAF near Star Lane were blown back and killed five people.

The war memorial was updated with the names of 82 men and one woman who lost their lives in the Second World War, inscribed on four stone tablets and unveiled at a dedication service on 17 October 1998.

Post-War

After the war, the experimentation and testing activities of the War Department became exclusive to the New Ranges, and was involved in the testing of components of Britain's earliest atomic bombs. The original garrison site focused on the training of troops, with artillery units in residence. During the early 1950s five officers' houses were built facing the east side of the cricket pitch and there were similar houses in Ness Road.

In the village itself, there was little development in the immediate post-war period, notable exceptions being Armagh and Antrim Roads.

The transitory nature of the garrison population caused inconvenience for the local schools and in 1955 Hinguar Street reported that it was not unusual for 70 of the 240 children on the school roll to leave and be replaced in any one year.

147 Ness Road. Ness Road was widened in 1930, involving the demolition of the building standing on the site of the original Well House.

148 Shoebury Common, full of summer visitors. The *Southend Standard* reported in June 1928: 'Over Whitsun, scores of tents were pitched along Southend Front between Thorpe Hall Avenue and Shoebury Common by sleepers-out.'

Weather

Saturday 31 January 1953 saw a high tide of seven feet above the predicated level. There were many breaches in the sea wall around Shoebury and extensive flooding to Foulness, the other islands and the New Ranges. Water flowed down Ness Road and flooded the marshes in the Old Ranges as far as Campfield Road. Although three people on Foulness lost their lives that night, casualties were far fewer than on Canvey Island or at Jaywick. The local casualties were two ladies and War Department constable S. Gray, who was on duty that night.

In the following weeks, the military amphibious vehicle was put to good use in rescue operations. Parties set out from Shoeburyness every day and worked from dawn to dark soaked to the skin through rescuing animals, securing property and sandbagging the sea walls. Lily Jerram–Burrows wrote that Shoebury people

'owe so much to the bravery and selflessness of the officers and men at the garrison'. It was many months before the Ranges, or indeed any businesses in the area, were back in full working order. The sea walls were subsequently raised.

1958 was one of exceptional snowfall, with Shoeburyness buried under a layer 23 inches thick. During the hard winter of 1962–3 (the coldest in Essex since 1740), the seashore between Southend and Shoeburyness was frozen solid. At Shoeburyness the ice stretched 650 feet out to sea and wind gusted at 75 mph.

Maplin Airport

During the 1960s the Maplin Sands were cited as an ideal location for a new international airport and possibly a seaport. The proposals became a hugely controversial issue, hotly debated across Essex and Kent. Public opposition came particularly from conservationists worried about seabirds and rare marshland eco-systems.

149   Another busy day at Shoebury Common, *c.*1950.

Two million pounds were spent on tests and studies but, in 1974, the scheme was finally abandoned. The sands are now a protected wildlife sanctuary, famed for its Brent Geese and tern population.

Manor Houses

North Shoebury Hall Farm, then owned by Southend-on-Sea Estates, had been farmed since 1966 by Roy Millbank, along with Tithe Farm, now in Great Wakering but created from fields formerly belonging to North Shoebury House. North Shoebury Hall itself had stood empty for some time when it burnt down in June 1968. The remaining farm buildings, then a motley collection of brick, wooden and iron sheds and barns, were demolished in December 1980 when the land was approved for development. Miraculously, the impressive barn built by Christopher

Parsons survived and was converted into a public house.

The town might also have lost South Shoebury Hall but for the foresight of Mrs M. Townend. In 1929 Captain and Mrs Townend took a 20-year lease on the house and 20 acres of land, then owned by Major Burges. They opened a poultry farm and the house benefited from much needed attention. The lease was subsequently extended for an additional 25 years, with the house scheduled for demolition at its expiry (1974). However, Mrs Townend purchased the freehold at the end of the lease, for which the town, and indeed the borough, should be eternally grateful. Captain Townend had died in 1965 and a weather vane was erected on St Andrew's to his memory.

After Townend's death 15 acres of fields, stretching down to the Shore House, were used as a caravan park until 1973 when sold for development by the Burges estate and is now the site of Freemantle and Admiral's Walk.

1960s-'70s

During the 1960s, older properties between West and Ness Roads (the first Cambridge Town houses) were replaced with council flats. The Eastern Avenue extension from Hamstel Road to Bournes Green was complete by the early 1970s, and the land between Thorpe Bay and Shoebury was further developed, until the two met at Maplin Way (formerly an old brickyard road, leading to landing stages on the beach). Although the residents gained easy access to the facilities of Southend, it was the beginning of the end for the rural character of North Shoebury.

Quarrying of brickearth was still carried out in the 1970s north-east of St Mary's, although Vanguards industrial estate was built on the brickworks site south of Elm Road. Towerfields industrial estate was also built at this time. This period saw many of Shoebury's elm trees lost to disease.

When Friars Farm in the High Street was sold by Mrs Eva Mott in 1919 for £1,460 it was described as a five-bedroomed, 'old-fashioned detached residence … matured garden with tennis lawn … stable and coach house'.

However, in 1974 it was demolished and replaced with six houses and four bungalows. Its fields were developed for housing throughout the '80s, although Friars Park remains a green oasis, popular with birdwatchers. Similarly, Shoebury Park, north of Elm Road, provides 20 acres of open space.

During the late 1970s-'80s, Southend-on-Sea Estates developed 150 acres of land east of North Shoebury Road and south of Poynters Lane, including 1,250 new homes. Named after Friars Farm, the development included playing fields, a new primary school and shops. Eagle Way, Hermes Way, and others were named after Second World War ships and laid out to

150 Shoebury Hall Farm caravan site, now covered by Admirals Walk and Freemantle. St Andrew's is just visible through the trees; the Sunshine Home is back right.

separate pedestrians from traffic where possible. Development rapidly continued with the Painters Estate, designed with different styles of housing north and south of Constable Way and, again, with efforts towards residential 'neighbourhoods', separated from through-traffic.

These estates added 2-3,000 residents to Shoebury and Richard Baker, the Hon. Secretary of the Rochford Hundred Historical Society, lamented this 'new, small town' to be the end of the 'last rural corner' of Southend.

In 1974, Essex local government was reorganised with all the existing urban districts and rural districts replaced with a new County Council and 14 District Councils. Shoeburyness remained part of Southend Council throughout this reorganisation and when Southend became a Unitary Authority in 1981, and by the end of the century had been divided into two local wards: Shoeburyness and West Shoebury.

The End of Shoebury Garrison

From 1948-71 gunner units had retained a presence at Shoeburyness, replaced by infantry battalions between 1971-6. The last resident unit was 1 battalion, the Duke of Edinburgh's Regiment.

151 The Sunshine Home, Ness Road was built for the deprived children of East and West Ham in 1929. South-end-on-Sea Hospital Management Committee took it over in 1952. In 1962 it was renamed Shoebury Hospital, becoming used exclusively for the care of the elderly until 1974.

The garrison HQ at Shoeburyness was finally disbanded in 1976, the residential artillery units relocated and the site abandoned. Properties around Campfield Road and the west gate were sold in 1978-9 and the Customs and Excise VAT computer centre was built on the site. Many non-residential structures on the garrison site were demolished.

Grove House and the water pumping and generating station were demolished and replaced by an Amstrad factory (1984). Soldiers' quarters (the 'Birdcages') were converted into flats off Rosewood Lane and the families' hospital in Campfield Road became the *Captain Mannering* pub. From 1986 a large area of marshes was leased to Southend Borough Council and opened as Gunners Park.

The New Ranges continued to be used for weapons-trials. The Proof and Experimental Establishment became part of the Defence Evaluation and Research Agency (DERA) in the mid-1980s, the Land and Maritime Ranges in 1994 and, in 1995, part of Defence Test and Evaluation Organisation (DTEO).

In 1997 the decision was taken to sell off the whole of the Old Ranges and in 1998 much of the work at Shoeburyness was transferred to Eskmeals in Cumbria. The closing of the Horseshoe Barracks was marked with a Sunset Ceremony on 4 March 1998, with music performed by the band of the Royal Regiment of Artillery and a static display by the Shoeburyness Branch of the Royal Artillery Association and the guns of 100th (Yeomanry) Regiment Royal Artillery (Volunteers). The salute was taken by Field Marshal The Lord Vincent, GBE KCB DSO; the senior military officer at Shoeburyness at the time was Lieutenant Colonel E. Happé RA.

The garrison site was eventually sold for development in 2000 in accordance with a planning brief agreed with Southend Borough Council. The purchaser, Gladedale Homes, was one of five developers to bid for the site.

Many of the surviving buildings are listed and much of the garrison has been designated as a conservation area. New flats on the site won a Design Award in 2005.

1980s-'90s Development

Following much debate, an Asda superstore opened on North Shoebury Road in 1981 and must take some responsibility for the continuing demise of South Shoebury's traditional shopping areas.

Fields formerly belonging to White House Farm and Moat House were developed by Southend-on-Sea Estates between 1981-88, forming the Bishopsteignton Estate, with streets named after Devonshire villages. In practice, the area comprises a collection of mini-estates, each constructed by different builders. The estate was marketed as a suburb of Thorpe Bay, despite being in Shoeburyness, and attracted more affluent members of the community. Property prices averaged £75,000 in 1982, compared with £35,000 east of North Shoebury Road. The White House itself, now a listed building, sold in 1981 for close to £150,000. Towards the end of the 1980s, Ravendale Way, Churchfields, and others were developed on former North Shoebury House land.

In 1981 the Pyghtle Cottage was described as 'a charming old-world cottage, beautifully maintained, and a pretty sight at the end of the path from the church'. Less than ten years later, a dilapidated, vandalised ruin, it was pulled down.

During the October 1987 hurricane, wind speeds of 60 knots were measured from 3am-6am at Shoeburyness. At 4.50am a gust of 87 knots was recorded – exactly 100mph, the strongest wind ever recorded in Essex. Here, as in much of Essex, roofs were lifted and chimney pots lost. Boats were hurled out of the water onto the beach, beach huts were smashed and the Commandant's conservatory was completely destroyed.

The Shoebury area suffered again on 18 September 1992 when a freak storm directly overhead measured 20mm of rain and wind

152   High Street, *c.*1940.

153   South end of the High Street, looking south.

up to 35 knots. Thousands of migrating birds at Foulness were killed by inch-thick hailstones. The storm raged for more than four hours and left a trail of devastation.

Residential development in 1992 filled the site of the old workhouse and Pyghtle Cottage north of St Mary's. At the time of writing, further residential development is planned east of North Shoebury Road, behind Asda.

Conservation

In 1981 part of the garrison and the adjacent High Street were identified by the Secretary of State for the Environment as having special architectural or historic interest and were designated a conservation area. The area includes the *Shoeburyness Hotel*, Nos 3-35 (odd) High Street and Nos 2-28 (even) High Street and the site of Nos 20-21 Rampart Street. On the garrison site itself, all the properties in Chapel Road including the unique Horseshoe Barracks, gatehouse and clock tower, garrison church of St Peter and St Paul, gunnery drill shed and the Long Course officers' quarters are within the conservation area. In addition, the Officers' Mess with its splendid oak-panelled dining room, Commandant's House, all the properties along The Terrace and Nos 1-5 Warrior Square Road are among the protected properties.

The Cold War Defence Boom and the Mulberry Harbour (accidentally dropped in the Thames off Shoebury during the Second World War) are protected as scheduled ancient monuments.

North Shoebury post office and shop at Parsons Corner closed in 1977. By 1988, the buildings stood derelict, despite their listed status. Planning permission was granted for conversion to a public house and the *Angel Inn* opened in the early 1990s. Philip Benton's birthplace, North Shoebury House, White House, Moat House, New Farm, Red Brick House and North Shoebury vicarage (marketed in 2006 for in excess of £2m), all now private family homes, are also listed buildings. Suttons, still owned by the military, is also listed, as is Parsons Barn, now a public house.

In 1999 Southend Council negotiated for the freehold of Gunners Park, and secured over 84 acres for the public. Part of the park, described as 'rough grassland and scrub' is now a designated Site of Special Scientific Interest, managed by the Essex Wildlife Trust. In addition, the mudflats off Shoebury, including Maplin Sands, have been identified as being of international importance as wintering grounds for waders and wildfowl.

One building apparently not worth conserving was the *Duke of Cambridge* pub, then under the name of *Shoe & Cobbler*, which was sold for redevelopment in 1999.

The landlord of the *Shoeburyness Hotel* pulled his last pint in 2004 and the listed building stood vacant for two years while developers haggled over planning permission. Residential development was eventually agreed.

From the 1970s to 2000 the population of Shoeburyness more than trebled.

In 2001 the population of West Shoebury Ward was 10,017 and that of Shoeburyness Ward

154   Officers' Mess awaiting redevelopment, 2006.

9,974. Many workers commute to Southend, Basildon, Chelmsford and London.

Shoebury has retained a strong character of its own over the centuries, from settlement site through defence point and military headquarters to the last rural corner of Southend Borough. Although outwardly now subsumed by Southend, Shoebury's unique location and fascinating history ensure that this will always be a special place.

155   New housing under construction on the garrison site, 2006.

Select Bibliography

Barry, P., *Shoeburyness and the Guns* (1965)

Benton, Philip, *The History of the Rochford Hundred* (1886–88)

Burrows, J.W., *Southend-on-Sea and District* (1909)

Currie, Ian, Davison, Mark and Ogley, Bob, *The Essex Weather Book* (1992)

Essex Review, Vol. XIX 1910; Vol. XV (1906)

Evans, H. Muir, *A Short History of the Thames Estuary* (undated)

Foley, Michael, *Front-line Essex* (2005)

Glennie, Donald, *Our Town – An Encyclopaedia of Southend-on-Sea & District* (1947)

Gordon, Dee, *People Who Mattered in Southend and Beyond* (2006)

Grimwood, Bob, *The Cinemas of Essex* (1995)

Hill, Tony, *Guns and Gunners at Shoeburyness* (1999)

Jerram–Burrows, L., *The History of the Rochford Hundred, South Shoebury* (1978)

King, W.H., *Ecclesiae Excensis* (1847, 1865)

Martin, Chris, *Shoeburyness* (1982)

Morant, P., *The History and Antiquities of the County of Essex, 1763-68* (1978)

Nash, Fred, 'World War Two Defences in Essex Project' in *Essex Archaeology and History* (2001)

Orford, Maureen, *The Shoebury Story* (2000)

Pollitt, William, *The Archaeology of the Rochford Hundred & South-East Essex* (1935)

Ryan, Pat, *Brick in Essex* (1999)

Smith, Graham, *Smuggling in Essex* (2005)

Smith, J.R., *Philip Benton, Gentleman Farmer and Antiquarian* (1991)

Smith, Ken, *Essex Under Arms* (1998)

Stibbards, Phyl, *The Listed Buildings of the Shoebury Area* (1988)

Urban District of Shoeburyness Official Guide, 1931

Wymer, J. and Brown, N., *North Shoebury: Settlement and Economy in South-East Essex* 1500 BC-AD 1500 (1995)

Yearsley, Ian, *Essex Events* (1999)

Index

References that relate to illustrations only are given in **bold**